Seventh Edition

THE MINNESOTA NOTARY LAW PRIMER

All the hard-to-find information every Minnesota Notary Public needs to know!

National Notary Association

Published by:

National Notary Association
9350 De Soto Avenue
Chatsworth, CA 91311-4926
Telephone: (800) 876-6827
Fax: (818) 700-0920
Website: www.NationalNotary.org
Email: nna@NationalNotary.org

©2015 National Notary Association
ALL RIGHTS RESERVED. No part of this book may be reproduced in any form without permission in writing from the publisher.

The information in this *Primer* is correct and current at the time of its publication, although new laws, regulations and rulings may subsequently affect the validity of certain sections. This information is provided to aid comprehension of state Notary Public requirements and should not be construed as legal advice. Please consult an attorney for inquiries relating to legal matters.

Seventh Edition ©2015
First Edition ©2004

ISBN: 978-1-59767-163-7

Table of Contents

Introduction 1

Notary Laws Explained 2

    The Notary Commission 2

    Official Notarial Acts 8

    Practices and Procedures 22

    Electronic Notarization 50

    Misconduct, Fines and Penalties 54

Minnesota Laws Pertaining to Notaries Public 58

About the NNA 91

Index 93

Have a Tough Notary Question?
If you were a National Notary Association member, you could get the answer to that difficult question. Join the NNA® and your membership includes access to the NNA® Hotline* and live Notary experts providing the latest Notary information regarding laws, rules and regulations.

Hours
Monday – Friday   5:00 a.m.–7:00 p.m. (PT)
Saturday   5:00 a.m.–5:00 p.m. (PT)

NNA® Hotline Toll-Free Phone Number: 1-888-876-0827

After hours you can leave a message or email our experts at Hotline@NationalNotary.org and they will respond the next business day.

*Access to the NNA® Hotline is for National Notary Association members and NNA® Hotline subscribers only. Call and become a member today.

Introduction

We commend you on your interest in Minnesota Notary law! Purchasing *The Minnesota Notary Law Primer* identifies you as a conscientious professional who takes your official responsibilities seriously.

In few fields is the expression "more to it than meets the eye" more true than in Notary law. What often appears on the surface to be a simple procedure may, in fact, have important legal considerations. *The Minnesota Notary Law Primer* is a resource created to help you decipher the state laws that affect notarization as well as to acquaint you with prudent Notary practices in general.

The Minnesota Notary Law Primer takes you through the myriad of Notary laws and puts them in easy-to-understand terms. Every section of the law is analyzed and explained, as well as topics not covered by Minnesota law but nonetheless of vital concern to you as a Notary.

For your convenience, we have reprinted the complete text of the laws of Minnesota that relate to Notaries Public.

Whether you're about to be commissioned for the first time or are a longtime Notary, we're sure that *The Minnesota Notary Law Primer* will provide you with new insight into and understanding of your official duties. Your improved comprehension of Minnesota's Notary laws will naturally result in your greater competence as a professional Notary Public.

> Milton G. Valera
> Chairman
> National Notary Association

Notary Laws Explained

In layperson's language, this chapter discusses and clarifies the laws of Minnesota that regulate Notaries Public. These laws are reprinted in "Minnesota Laws Pertaining to Notaries Public" beginning on page 58.

Most provisions cited are from Chapters 357, 358, 359 and 507 of the Minnesota Statutes (MS). However, other applicable citations are listed, as are references to materials on the Secretary of State's website.

Additional information about Minnesota's requirements for Notaries Public is available on the Secretary's website. For step-by-step instructions on the commission application process, applicants also may go to *www.nationalnotary.org/minnesota/become-a-notary*.

THE NOTARY COMMISSION

Notary Oversight

<u>Appointment, Recordkeeping and Oversight of Notaries</u>. In Minnesota, Notaries are appointed by the Governor, with the advice and consent of the Senate. The Secretary of State handles the administrative tasks associated with issuance and maintenance of commissions (MS 359.01[1]). The Commissioner of Commerce investigates complaints and allegations of misconduct against Notaries (MS 359.02 and 359.12).

Application for Commission

<u>Qualifications for Residents</u>. To become a Notary in Minnesota, the applicant must meet each of the following criteria (MS 359.01[1]):

- Be at least 18 years old

- Be a citizen or permanent resident of Minnesota

Qualifications for Nonresidents. Applicants who are residents of Iowa, North Dakota, South Dakota or Wisconsin are eligible to hold a Minnesota Notary commission (MS 359.01[2][a][1]). Nonresident Notaries must designate the Minnesota county in which their Notary commission will be recorded (MS 359.01[2][a][3]). Nonresident Notaries also must designate the Secretary of State as their agent for the service of process for all purposes relating to notarial acts and for receipt of all correspondence relating to notarial acts (MS 359.01[2][a][2]).

Ex Officio Notaries. The following officers have the powers of a Notary Public in Minnesota (MS 358.15[a]):

- Members of the legislature, while still residing in the district from which they were elected

- The clerks or recorders of towns and cities

- Court commissioners, county recorders and county auditors, and their several deputies, and county commissioners, all within their respective counties

- Peace officers licensed under MS 626.845, who are authorized to administer oaths and affirmations

Qualifying Questions. An applicant must answer the following questions on the application and provide written explanation and copies of legal documentation if any answer is "yes" (website, "Notary Commission Application"):

- Have you ever been the subject of any inquiry or investigation with respect to a Notary commission or by any division of the Minnesota Commerce Department?

- Have you ever had a professional license censured, revoked, suspended, canceled or terminated, or have you been the subject of any type of administrative action in any state?

- Have you ever been charged with, convicted of, indicted for or entered a plea to any crime other than a traffic violation?

- Have you ever been a defendant in any lawsuit alleging fraud, misrepresentation, conversion, mismanagement of funds, breach of fiduciary duty or breach of contract?

Application. Each applicant must complete the official application provided by the Secretary of State. The application includes the Notary's oath of office. The application is available at the following address:

> Minnesota Secretary of State — Notary
> Retirement Systems Building of Minnesota
> 60 Empire Drive, Suite 100
> Saint Paul, MN 55103-2141
> (651) 296-2803 or (877) 551-6767
> https://notary.sos.state.mn.us/

Oath of Office. Every Minnesota Notary is required to take an official oath that he or she will support the constitutions of the United States and of Minnesota, and will honestly and discharge the duties of the Notary office to the best of his or her judgment and ability. (MS 358.05 and Minnesota Constitution, Article V, Section 6.) The oath of office is a written statement included on the application for commission (website, "Notary Commission Application").

Application Fee. The fee for a Notary commission application is $120 (MS 359.01[3][a]).

Recording the Commission. Once the Notary commission has been issued, a resident Notary must register the commission with either the office of the local registrar of the Notary's county of residence or other county department assigned under MS 485.27 to handle Notary administration in the Notary's county of residence. At the same time, the Notary also must submit a sample of his or her signature. The signature must match the first, middle and last names on the Notary's commission and Notary stamp and must be signed in the style that the Notary plans to use when performing notarizations (MS 359.061[1]).

A nonresident Notary must register his or her commission and signature with the court administrator of the district court or county department that handles Notary administration in the Minnesota county that the nonresident Notary designates (MS 359.061[2]).

The fee to register the commission and signature is $20 for both residents and nonresidents (MS 357.021[2][12] and website, "Notary Commission Application").

Notary Stamp. After receiving and registering his or her commission, the Notary applicant must purchase an official rubber stamp. (See "Notary Stamp," pages 35–38.)

Notary Bond

Not Required. Minnesota Notaries are not now required to obtain a surety bond. However, some employers may require a Notary to obtain a bond or insurance (website, "Notary Commission Guide").

Liability. As ministerial officials, Notaries may be held financially responsible for any and all damages caused by their mistakes or misconduct in performing notarial acts. If a person is financially injured by a Notary's negligence or failure to properly execute a notarial act — whether performed intentionally or unintentionally — the Notary may be sued in civil court and ordered to pay all resulting damages, including attorneys' fees.

A person need not be named in a document in order to sue a Notary for damages resulting from the Notary's handling of that document. If, for example, a lender accepts a forged, notarized deed as collateral for a loan, the lender might sue to recover losses from the Notary who witnessed the bogus deed.

Errors and Omissions Insurance. Notaries may choose to purchase insurance to cover any unintentional errors or omissions they may make. Notary errors and omissions insurance provides protection for Notaries who are involved in claims or sued for damages resulting from unintentional notarial errors and omissions. In the event of a claim or civil lawsuit, the insurance company will provide and pay for the Notary's legal counsel and absorb any damages levied by a court or agreed to in a settlement, up to the policy coverage limit. Generally, errors and omissions insurance does not cover the Notary for dishonest, fraudulent or criminal acts or omissions, or for willful or intentional disregard of the law.

Jurisdiction

Statewide. Notaries may perform official acts throughout the state of Minnesota but not beyond the state borders (MS 359.04). A Notary may not witness the signing of a document outside of Minnesota and then return to the state to perform the notarization. All parts of a notarial act must be performed at the same time and place within the state of Minnesota.

Term of Office

Five-Year Term. A Minnesota Notary holds office until January 31st of the fifth year following the year the commission was issued (MS 359.02).

Change of Address

Notification. Whenever a Notary changes his or her principal business, residence or mailing address, the Notary must submit written notice of the change to the Secretary of State's office within 30 days (MS 359.071). A Notary whose address has changed may print the "Notification of Address Change for Notary Public" form from the Secretary of State's website, and complete and mail the form. Alternatively, a Notary may log in to his or her "Notary Commission Application" in the Notary Online System, check the "Address Change" box, and enter the new information electronically. There is no fee for notification of an address change (website, "Change Name or Address").

Moving to a New County. If a Notary residing in the state of Minnesota changes a residence address to a new county, the Notary must submit written notice to the Secretary of State and reregister his or her commission and signature with the local registrar in the new county of residence (The Notary should contact his or her new county offices to find out where to go to reregister the commission and whether a fee must be paid. (website, "Notary Commission Application").

Change of Name

Notification. Whenever a Notary changes his or her name, the Notary must submit written notice of the change to the Secretary of State's office within 30 days (MS 359.071). There is no fee for notification of a name change (website, "Notary Commission Application").

Procedure. The Notary must notify the Secretary of State's office of a name change by completing a new "Notary Commission Application" form and attaching his or her commission certificate and documentation of the legal name change (e.g., court documents or a marriage certificate).

Once the Notary receives the commission in the new name, the Notary must register his or her new commission and signature with the local registrar in the county in which the Notary resides (website, "Notary Commission Application"). The Notary must also purchase a new Notary stamp reflecting the change in name. (See "Notary Stamp," pages 35–38.)

Nonresidents. Nonresident Notaries must register their new signatures in the Minnesota county in which they were appointed (website, "Notary Commission Application").

Reappointment

Procedure. Effective July 31, 2011, a Notary may renew his or her commission six months before the expiration of the current commission. Previously a Notary could apply for reappointment only within 60 days before the expiration of the commission. A Notary whose commission has expired may apply for reappointment any time after the commission expiration date (MS 359.02). Notaries will not, however, be automatically reappointed. A Notary who wishes to renew his or her commission must complete an application in the same manner as first-time applicants (website, "Notary Commission Application"), submitting the $120 application fee (MS 359.01[3][a]) and the $20 fee to register the commission (MS 357.021[2][12]).

Renewals may now be submitted online. E-check or credit card (Visa and MasterCard) payments are accepted for online applications. If renewing by mail, a check or money order payable to the "Office of the Secretary of State" is the only acceptable method of payment (website, "Frequently Asked Questions").

Notary Stamp. Renewing Notaries also must purchase a new rubber stamp (website, "Frequently Asked Questions"). (See "Notary Stamp, pages 35–38.)

Resignation

Procedure. Should a Notary Public wish to resign the commission, he or she should first contact the Secretary of State's office online at notary.sos@state.mn.us, or by calling 651-296-2803 or 1-877-551-6767. The Notary will be instructed to send a signed letter of resignation to the office of the Secretary of State. The resignation is considered effective once the letter is received, unless an effective date is indicated (MS 351.01). The National Notary Association recommends the notice of resignation be sent by certified mail.

Since the Minnesota Statutes do not prescribe rules for the disposition of the Notary's official stamp and journal upon resignation, the National Notary Association recommends that a resigning Notary destroy or deface the stamp to prevent fraudulent use and safely store all journals for a period of at least 10 years from the date of the last entry in the journal.

Withdrawing Resignation. A resignation may be withdrawn if written notice is sent to the appropriate person or agency either before the requested effective date or before the person or agency accepts the resignation (MS 351.01).

OFFICIAL NOTARIAL ACTS

Authorized Acts

Notaries may perform the following notarial acts (MS 358.42, 359.04, 359.085 and 359.11):

- Acknowledgments, certifying that a signer personally appeared before the Notary, was positively identified by the Notary and acknowledged signing the document. (See pages 10–13.)

- Signature Witnessings, certifying that the signer personally appeared before the Notary, was positively identified by the Notary and signed the document in the Notary's presence. (See pages 13–14.)

- Oaths and Affirmations, witnessing solemn promises to a Supreme Being (oaths) or solemn promises on one's own personal honor (affirmations). (See pages 14–16.)

- Verifications Upon Oath or Affirmation (Jurats), certifying that the signer personally appeared before the Notary, was positively identified by the Notary, signed the document in the Notary's presence and took an oath or affirmation. (See pages 16–17.)

- Depositions, certifying that the spoken words of a witness in a legal matter were accurately taken down in writing, most often made by skilled court reporters. (See page 18.)

- Copy Certifications, attesting that a photocopy of a document, which is not a vital or public record, is a true, accurate and complete replication of the original document. (See pages 19–21.)

- Protests, certifying that a written promise to pay, such as a bill of exchange, was not honored. (See pages 21–22.)

Unauthorized Acts

Execute Proofs of Execution by Subscribing Witness. Minnesota law does not allow Notaries to perform proofs of execution by subscribing witness. In a proof of execution, the subscribing witness appearing before a Notary in place of an absent document signer swears or affirms that he or she witnessed the signing of a document by, or took the acknowledgment of, the absent document signer.

Notarize Own Signature. A Notary may not acknowledge or witness or attest to his or her own signature. Furthermore, a Notary may not take a verification of his or her own oath or affirmation (MS 359.085[7]).

Notarize Document in Which Notary Named. The Secretary of State considers a Notary who notarizes a document in which the Notary is named to be acting unlawfully under MS 359.12, which prohibits Notaries from the dishonest and unfaithful discharge of their notarial duties (website, "Frequently Asked Questions").

Complete False Certificate. A Notary may not complete a Notary certificate that contains information the Notary knows to be false (MS 609.65).

Certify Copies of Vital or Public Records. A Notary is not authorized to certify a copy of a document that is a vital or public record or is publicly recordable (website, "Notary Commission Guide").

MINNESOTA NOTARY LAW PRIMER

Practice Law. A nonattorney Notary may not give legal advice to a document signer or prepare any legal document — especially not for a fee (MS 481.02[1]). This includes assisting a signer in completing, selecting or understanding a document or transaction.

Perform Marriage Ceremonies. Minnesota Notaries may not perform wedding ceremonies unless they are also clergy members or officials granted power to solemnize marriages.

Acknowledgments

Definition. An acknowledgment is a notarial act in which a document signer personally appears before a Notary, is identified by the Notary as the person named in the document, and admits (or "acknowledges") to the Notary that he or she signed the document for the purposes stated in it.

The signer may be signing as an individual, acting on his or her own behalf, or in a representative capacity, acting on behalf of an entity or another person. When a signer is acting in a representative capacity, the signer also acknowledges that he or she has the proper authority to sign in the stated capacity.

Purpose. Acknowledgments are one of the most common forms of notarization. Typically, they are executed on deeds and other documents that will be publicly recorded by a county official. The primary purpose of an acknowledgment is to positively identify the document signer.

In executing an acknowledgment, a Notary certifies three things:

1) The signer *personally appeared* before the Notary on the date and in the county indicated on the Notary certificate. Notarization cannot be based on a telephone call or on a Notary's familiarity with a signature.

2) The Notary *positively identified* the signer through either personal knowledge or satisfactory evidence. (See "Identifying Document Signers," pages 22–26).

3) The signer *acknowledged* to the Notary that the signature is his or hers and was freely made for the purposes stated in the document. If a document is willingly signed in the presence of the Notary, this can serve just as well as an oral statement of acknowledgment.

NOTARY LAWS EXPLAINED

Identification of Acknowledger. In taking an acknowledgment, the Notary must identify the signer through one of three methods of satisfactory evidence: personal knowledge, a credible identifying witness or identification documents (MS 358.42 and 359.085). (See "Identifying Document Signers," pages 22–26.)

Terminology. In discussing the notarial act of acknowledgment, it is important to use the proper terminology. A Notary takes or executes an acknowledgment, while a document signer makes or gives an acknowledgment.

Witnessing Signature Not Required. For an acknowledgment, the document does not have to be signed in the Notary's presence. As long as the signer appears before the Notary at the time of the notarization to acknowledge having signed, the Notary may execute the acknowledgment.

In most states, a document could be signed an hour before, a week before, a year before, etc. — as long as the signer appears before the Notary with the signed document at the time of notarization to admit that the signature is his or her own.

Representative Capacity. Representative capacity is the authority to sign a document on the behalf, or as the representative, of another person, organization or entity. Under Minnesota law, a person may sign and acknowledge a document in a representative capacity under the following conditions (MS 358.41[4]):

- for and on behalf of a corporation, partnership, limited liability company, trust or other entity, as an authorized officer, agent, partner, trustee or other representative

- as a public officer, personal representative, guardian or other representative in the specific capacity described in the document

- as an attorney in fact for an absent principal signer

- in any other lawful capacity as an authorized representative of another

Minnesota law does not require the Notary to verify the signer's representative status. If the Notary does not have personal

11

MINNESOTA NOTARY LAW PRIMER

knowledge of the signer's capacity, however, it is a prudent practice to request proof of his or her authority to sign.

Minnesota law requires an individual signing for a principal signer as attorney in fact to disclose his identity as attorney in fact and to sign in substantially the following manner: "Signature by a person as 'attorney in fact for (name of the principal)' or '(name of principal) by 'name of the attorney in fact) the principal's attorney in fact'.

An acknowledgment made in a representative capacity on behalf of a corporation, partnership, trust or other entity and notarized with the representative certificate wording prescribed by law is *prima facie* evidence that the document was executed with proper authority (MS 358.50). *"Prima facie"* evidence is evidence presented in court that is sufficient to create a presumption of fact or to establish the fact unless rebutted.

Certificate for Married Persons. If a husband and wife acknowledge the execution of a document together, and at the same time, they shall be described in the acknowledgment certificate as husband and wife. If each spouse acknowledges his or her signature before a different Notary, or before the same Notary at different times, each shall be described in the certificate as the spouse of the other (MS 358.14).

Certificates for Acknowledgment. Minnesota law provides certificate wording for acknowledgments by persons signing in individual and representative capacities (MS 358.48).

- For an individual signing on his or her own behalf (MS 358.48[1]):

    State of Minnesota
    County of _____

    This instrument was acknowledged before me on _____ (date) by _____ (name[s] of person[s]).

    _____
    (Signature of notarial officer)

    Title (and Rank) _____   (Stamp)

    My commission expires: _____

- For an individual signing in a representative capacity (MS 358.48[2]):

    State of Minnesota
    County of _____

    This instrument was acknowledged before me on _____ (date) by _____ (name[s] of person[s]) as _____ (type of authority, e.g., officer, trustee, etc.) of _____ (name of party on behalf of whom the instrument was executed).

    _____
    (Signature of notarial officer)

    Title (and Rank) _____   (Stamp)

    My commission expires: _____

Signature Witnessings

Purpose. In a signature witnessing, the Notary determines the signer's identity through satisfactory evidence and witnesses the signer sign in the way he or she is named in the document (MS 358.42[c]).

Witnessing a signature may be used in circumstances where the date of signing is of crucial importance. A signature witnessing differs from an acknowledgment in that the party relying upon the document knows that the document was signed on a certain date. A signature witnessing differs from a verification in that the signer is merely signing the document, not vouching that the contents of the document are true.

In a signature witnessing, the Notary certifies the following:

- The signer personally appeared before the Notary at the time of notarization on the date and in the county indicated. (Notarization based upon a phone call or on familiarity with a signature is not acceptable.)

- The signer was positively identified by the Notary through satisfactory evidence (see "Identifying Document Signers," pages 22–26).

Certificate for Signature Witnessing. The following wording is prescribed by law for a signature witnessing (MS 358.48[4]):

State of Minnesota
County of _____

Signed or attested before me on _____ (date) by
_____ (name[s]) of person[s]).

_____
(Signature of notarial officer)

Title (and Rank) _____   (Stamp)

My commission expires: _____

Oaths and Affirmations

Purpose. An oath is a solemn, spoken pledge to a Supreme Being. An affirmation is a solemn, spoken pledge on one's own personal honor, with no reference to a Supreme Being. Both are promises of truthfulness and have the same legal effect (MS 358.08, 358.09 and 359.04). In taking an oath or affirmation in an official proceeding, a person may be subject to criminal penalties for perjury should he or she fail to be truthful.

An oath or affirmation can be a full-fledged notarial act in its own right without an accompanying document, as when giving an oath of office to a public official (e.g., when swearing in a public official), or it can be part of the process of notarizing a document (e.g., executing a verification or swearing in a credible witness).

A person who objects to taking an oath may instead be given an affirmation, which does not refer to a Supreme Being (MS 358.08).

Power to Administer. Minnesota Notaries and certain other officers are authorized to administer oaths and affirmations and, if the oath or affirmation is in writing, to complete a certificate for it (MS 358.09 and 358.10).

Ceremony and Gestures. To impress upon the oath-taker or affirmant the importance of truthfulness, Minnesota law requires that the person swearing or affirming raise his or her right hand when taking the oath or affirmation (MS 358.09). The oath or affirmation must be spoken aloud, and the oath-taker or affirmant must respond affirmatively with the words "I do," "Yes" or the like. A nod or grunt is not a clear and sufficient response. If a person is unable to speak, the Notary may rely upon written notes to communicate.

<u>Wording for Oaths (Affirmations)</u>. Minnesota law contains oath forms for use in the following cases (MS 358.07):

- Oath to grand jurors

- Oath to petit jurors in civil actions

- Oath to petit jurors in criminal cases

- Oath to officers attending grand juries

- Oath to officers in charge of petit juries

- Oath to officers in charge during recess

- Oath to witnesses

- Oath to interpreters

- Oath to attorneys

- Oath to affiants

<u>Most Frequent Oath Forms</u>. The two statutory oath forms that Notaries are most likely to use are the following:

- Oath (affirmation) for an affiant signing an affidavit:

    You do swear that the statements of this affidavit, by you subscribed, are true. So help you God (MS 358.07[10]).

    (You do affirm that the statements of this affidavit, by you subscribed, are true, and this you do under the penalties of perjury [MS 358.07[10] and 358.08].)

- Oath (affirmation) for a witness testifying in a court case or giving a deposition:

   You do swear that the evidence you shall give relative to the cause now under consideration shall be the truth, the whole truth, and nothing but the truth. So help you God (MS 358.07[7]).

   (You do affirm that the evidence you shall give relative to the cause now under consideration shall be the truth, the whole truth, and nothing but the truth, and this you do under the penalties of perjury [MS 358.07[7] and 358.08].)

While Minnesota statute does not stipulate a specific oath to be administered to a credible witness who is identifying a document signer, a Notary may use the following wording:

- Oath (affirmation) for a credible identifying witness:

   You do swear that you personally know that this signer truly holds the identity he or she claims, so help you God.

   (You do affirm that you personally know that this signer truly holds the identity he or she claims, and this you do under the penalties of perjury.)

Verifications Upon Oath or Affirmation (Jurats)

Purpose. In notarizing signatures on affidavits, depositions and other forms of written verification requiring an oath or affirmation by the signer, the Notary must witness the signing of the document and administer an oath or affirmation to the signer, who must swear to or affirm the truthfulness of the statements in the document (MS 358.42[b] and 359.085[2]).

While the purpose of an acknowledgment is to positively identify a document signer, the purpose of a verification (or jurat) is to compel truthfulness by appealing to the signer's conscience and fear of criminal penalties for perjury. An acknowledgment is not an acceptable substitute for a verification. A Notary may not take an acknowledgment in lieu of administering an oath for a verification.

In executing a verification, a Notary certifies the following (MS 358.42 and 359.085):

1) The signer *personally appeared* before the Notary at the time of notarization on the date and in the county indicated on the Notary certificate. Notarization cannot be based on a telephone call or on a Notary's familiarity with a signature.

2) The Notary *positively identified* the signer through either personal knowledge or satisfactory evidence. See "Identifying Document Signers," pages 22–26.

3) The Notary watched the *signer sign the document* at the time of notarization.

4) The Notary *administered an oath or affirmation* to the signer.

Oath (Affirmation) for Verifications. Minnesota law prescribes the following oath (or affirmation) wording for the verification of an affidavit by an affiant:

You do swear that the statements of this affidavit, by you subscribed, are true. So help you God (MS 358.07[10]).

(You do affirm that the statements of this affidavit, by you subscribed, are true, and this you do under the penalties of perjury [MS 358.08[10] and 358.08].)

Certificate for a Verification (Jurat). The following short-form wording for a verification is prescribed by Minnesota law (MS 358.48[3]):

State of Minnesota
County of _____

Signed and sworn to (or affirmed) before me on _____ (date) by _____ (name[s] of person[s] making statement).

_____
(Signature of notarial officer)

Title (and Rank) _____   (Stamp)

My commission expires: _____

MS 358.09 provides alternate certificate wording for a verification (jurat): "Subscribed and sworn to before me this _____ day of _____, ____."

Depositions

Purpose. A deposition is a signed transcript of the signer's oral statements taken down for use in a judicial proceeding. The deposition signer is called the deponent.

With a deposition, both sides in a lawsuit or court case have the opportunity to cross-examine the deponent. Questions and answers are transcribed into a written statement. Used only in judicial proceedings, a deposition is then signed and sworn to before an oath-administering official (MS 359.04).

Procedure. Although Minnesota Notaries have the power to take depositions, this duty is most often executed by trained and certified shorthand reporters, also known as court reporters. The Notary's role is normally limited to administering the oath or affirmation to the deponent or notarizing the deponent's signature in the deposition.

In notarizing a deponent's signature on a deposition, the Notary typically administers an oath or affirmation and completes some form of verification, or jurat, which the Notary signs and authenticates by affixing an imprint of the official stamp.

Power to Compel Attendance. A Minnesota Notary has authority to compel witnesses to attend the deposition hearing and to punish witnesses for nonattendance or for refusing to testify in accordance with state law or court rule (MS 359.11).

Oath (Affirmation) for Depositions. Minnesota law prescribes the following oath (or affirmation) wording for a witness testifying in a court case or giving a deposition:

> You do swear that the evidence you shall give relative to the cause now under consideration shall be the truth, the whole truth, and nothing but the truth. So help you God (MS 358.07[7]).

> (You do affirm that the evidence you shall give relative to the cause now under consideration shall be the truth, the whole truth, and nothing but the truth, and this you do under the penalties of perjury [MS 358.07[7] and 358.08].)

Affidavits

Purpose. An affidavit is a signed statement made under oath or affirmation by a person called an affiant, and it is used for a variety of purposes, both in and out of court.

Affidavits are used to make sworn statements for many reasons, from declaring losses to an insurance company to declaring U.S. citizenship before traveling to a foreign country. An affidavit must be voluntarily signed and sworn to or affirmed before a Notary or other official with oath-administering powers. Unlike depositions, affidavits may be used both in and outside of court. If affidavits are used in a judicial proceeding, only one side in the case need participate, in contrast to the deposition.

Procedure. For an affidavit, the Notary must administer an oath or affirmation and complete some form of verification, which the Notary signs and authenticates by affixing an imprint of the official stamp.

In an affidavit, the Notary's certificate typically sandwiches the affiant's signed statement, with the venue and affiant's name at the top of the document and the jurat wording at the end. The Notary is responsible for the venue, affiant's name and any Notary text at the beginning and end of the affidavit. The affiant is responsible for the signed statement in the middle.

Certificate for Affidavits. Affidavits typically require jurat certificates. (See "Verifications Upon Oath or Affirmation," pages 16–17.)

Oath (Affirmation) for Affidavits. Minnesota law prescribes the following oath (or affirmation) wording for affiants:

> You do swear that the statements of this affidavit, by you subscribed, are true. So help you God (MS 358.07[10]).

> (You do affirm that the statements of this affidavit, by you subscribed, are true, and this you do under the penalties of perjury [MS 358.08].)

Copy Certifications

Purpose. Minnesota Notaries have the authority to certify that a transcribed copy or photocopy of a document, electronic record or other item is a complete and true reproduction of that which was copied (MS 358.42[d] and 359.085).

Notaries are commonly asked to certify copies of documents that people do not want to risk losing. Examples of documents that may lawfully be certified as true copies by a Notary include: a driver's license, a Social Security card, a medical record, a passport and a bill of sale.

MINNESOTA NOTARY LAW PRIMER

Original and Source Documents. While Minnesota statute permits Notaries to certify copies of documents, the statute does not require the documents to be originals, that is, documents containing a handwritten signature in pen and ink. The statute simply states that a Notary must determine that the copy presented is a full, true and accurate transcription or reproduction of "that which was copied." Thus, Notaries may certify a copy of an original document or instrument of writing or of any "source" document. For example, a Notary could lawfully certify a photocopy of a document as a true copy, if a photocopy and not the original was the source document.

Documents, Electronic Records and Other Items. Minnesota Notaries may certify as a true copy a transcription or reproduction of a "document, electronic record or other item." A document is any instrument of writing which may or may not contain a signature.

An electronic record is a document created using electronic means, and perhaps signed and notarized with electronic signatures (MS 358.41[7]).

The Notary may also certify a copy of an "item." While the statute does not define the term, an "item" may include a chart, diagram or other form of writing that may not properly be classified as a document. For example, a photocopy or transcribed copy of a chart depicting a family tree may be considered an item that may be certified as a true copy by a Notary.

Prohibited Documents. Notaries may not certify copies of recordable or recorded documents. A recordable document is an instrument that is typically filed with a county recorder but which has not yet been recorded, while a recorded document is a recordable document which has been filed. An individual who needs a certified copy of a recordable document, such as a deed, should first record the document and then have the recording agency provide a certified copy.

In addition, Notaries may not certify copies of vital records such as birth or death certificates. Only officials in a bureau of vital statistics or other public record office may certify originals or copies of such documents. A Notary's "certification" of such a copy may lend credibility to what is actually a counterfeit or altered document.

Procedure. The permanent custodian of the original document must present the source document, electronic record or other item to be copied to the Notary and request a certified copy. The Notary should make or closely supervise the making of the photocopy to ensure that it is a true and accurate copy of the source document, electronic record or other item.

If the person requesting the certified copy presents the source document and a transcribed copy (or a photocopy), the Notary must determine that the copy is a full, true and accurate copy of the original.

Certificate for Copy Certification. A Notary certificate attesting to the trueness of a copy should substantially comply with the following statutory form (MS 358.48[5]):

State of Minnesota
County of _____

I certify that this is a true and correct copy of a document in the possession of _____.

Dated: _____

_____
(Signature of notarial officer)

Title (and Rank) _____   (Stamp)

My commission expires: _____

Protests

Definition. A protest is a written statement by a Notary or other authorized officer, verifying that payment was not received on a negotiable instrument such as a bank draft. Failure to pay is called *dishonor*.

Before issuing a certificate of protest, the Notary must present the bank draft or other instrument to the person, firm, or institution obligated to pay, a procedure called *presentment*.

Purpose. The purpose of a protest is to evidence the dishonor of a negotiable instrument. The protest initiates the civil process of recovering the payment that was dishonored.

Antiquated Act. In the 19th century, protests were common notarial acts in the United States, but they are rarely performed today due to the advent of modern electronic communications and resulting changes in our banking and financial systems. Modern Notaries most often encounter protests in the context of international commerce.

Special Knowledge Required. Notarial acts of protest are complicated and varied, requiring a special knowledge of financial and legal terminology. State officials encourage Notaries to seek guidance from an attorney before performing this act.

PRACTICES AND PROCEDURES

Personal Appearance

Requirement. The principal signer must personally appear before the Notary at the time of the notarization. This means that the Notary and the signer must both be physically present, face to face in the same room, when the notarization takes place. Notarizations may never be performed over the telephone.

Willingness

Confirmation. Minnesota Notaries are required to confirm that the signer is acting willingly.

To confirm willingness, the Notary need only ask document signers if they are signing of their own free will. If a signer does or says anything that makes the Notary think the signer is being pressured to sign, it is best for the Notary to refuse to notarize.

Awareness

Confirmation. Minnesota Notaries are required to confirm that the signer is generally aware of what is happening and seems to understand the significance of the transaction.

To confirm awareness, the Notary simply makes a layperson's judgment about the signer's ability to understand what is taking place. A document signer who cannot respond intelligibly in a simple conversation with the Notary should not be considered sufficiently aware to sign at that moment. If the notarization is taking place in a medical environment, the signer's doctor can be consulted for a professional opinion. Otherwise, if the signer's awareness is in doubt, the Notary must refuse to notarize.

Identifying Document Signers

Satisfactory Evidence. In taking an acknowledgment or executing a jurat or signature witnessing, Minnesota law requires the Notary to positively identify the document signer using satisfactory evidence. The following are the three acceptable forms of satisfactory evidence (MS 358.42[f] and 359.085):

- The Notary's personal knowledge of the signer's identity (See "Personal Knowledge of Identity," below.)

- Reliable identification documents or ID cards (See "Identification Documents (ID Cards)," pages 23–25.)

- The oath or affirmation of one personally known credible identifying witness (See "Credible Identifying Witness," pages 25–26.)

Personal Knowledge of Identity

Definition. The safest and most reliable method of identifying a document signer is for the Notary to depend upon his or her own knowledge of the signer's identity. In order to use this method of identification, Minnesota statute requires that the Notary's knowledge of a signer must be personal (MS 358.42[f] and 359.085). That is, the Notary's familiarity or knowledge should be based upon interactions with that person over a period of time sufficient to eliminate every reasonable doubt that the person has the identity claimed.

Minnesota law does not specify how long a Notary must be acquainted with an individual before personal knowledge of identity may be claimed. Therefore, the Notary's common sense must prevail. In general, the longer the Notary is acquainted with a person, and the more random interactions the Notary has had with that person, the more likely it is that the individual is personally known.

For instance, the Notary might safely consider a friend since childhood as personally known, but would be foolish to regard a person met for the first time the previous day as such. Whenever the Notary has a reasonable doubt about a signer's identity, that individual should not be considered personally known, and the identification should be made through either credible identifying witnesses or reliable identification documents.

Identification Documents (ID Cards)

Purpose. Minnesota law states that a Notary has satisfactory evidence if the individual is identified on the basis of identification documents (MS 358.42[f] and 359.085).

Elements of Reliable Identification Documents. Minnesota law does not prescribe the characteristics for acceptable ID cards presented as satisfactory evidence. However, the National Notary Association recommends that any reliable ID document should meet the following criteria:

- Be current

- Be issued by a federal, state or tribal government, or national government in the case of a foreign passport

- Contain the bearer's photograph, signature and physical description (although a passport without a physical description is acceptable)

Reliable Identification Documents. The identification documents listed below meet the criteria for reliable identification documents and are commonly accepted by Minnesota Notaries to identify strangers:

- A Minnesota driver's license or non-driver's identification card issued by the Department of Public Safety Driver and Vehicle Services

- A driver's license or non-driver's ID from a foreign country or another U.S. state that meets the recommended criteria for an acceptable identification card

- A U.S. or foreign passport

- An identification card issued by a native American tribal government

- An identification card issued by the U.S. Citizenship and Immigration Services (USCIS)

Multiple Identification Documents. While one acceptable identification document or card may be sufficient to identify a signer, the Notary may ask for more.

Unacceptable Identification Documents. ID cards that are not acceptable for use in identifying signers include, but are not limited to, birth certificates, Social Security cards and credit cards.

Name Variations. The Notary must make sure that the name on the document is the same as the name appearing on the identification presented. In certain circumstances, it may be acceptable for the name on the document to be an abbreviated form of the name on the ID — for example, John D. Smith instead of John David Smith. Last names or surnames, however, should always be the same.

Fraudulent Identification Documents. Identification documents are the least secure of the three methods of identifying a document signer, because phony ID cards are common. The Notary should scrutinize each card for evidence of tampering or counterfeiting, or for evidence that it is a genuine card issued to an impostor.

Some clues that an ID card may have been fraudulently altered with include mismatched type styles, a photograph that is raised from the surface, a signature that does not match the signature on the document, unauthorized lamination of the card and smudges, erasures, smears and discolorations.

Possible tip-offs to a counterfeit ID card include misspelled words, a brand-new-looking card with an old date of issuance, two cards with exactly the same photograph and inappropriate patterns and textures.

Some possible indications that a card may have been issued to an impostor include the birth date or address printed on the card being unfamiliar to the bearer and all the ID cards seeming brand new.

Credible Identifying Witness

Purpose. When a document signer is not personally known to the Notary and is not able to present reliable identification documents, that signer may be identified on the oath (or affirmation) of a credible identifying witness who is unaffected by the transaction (MS 358.42[f]).

Qualifications. Each credible identifying witness should personally know the document signer. Also, the witness must be personally known by the Notary. This establishes a chain of personal knowledge from the signer to the credible identifying witness to the Notary. A credible identifying witness should have no beneficial interest in the transaction and have a reputation for honesty.

Credible Identifying Witness Oath. To ensure truthfulness, the Notary must administer an oath (or affirmation) to each credible identifying witness. An acceptable oath (affirmation) for a credible identifying witness might be:

> Do you solemnly swear that you personally know this signer truly holds the identity he (or she) claims, so help you God?
>
> (Do you solemnly, sincerely and truly declare and affirm that you personally know this signer truly holds the identity he (or she) claims, doing this under the pains and penalties of perjury?)

Signature in Notary's Journal. Notaries should record the printed name and address of each credible identifying witness and obtain each witness' signature in their official journal.

Journal of Notarial Acts

Recommended. Although Minnesota Notaries are not required by law to maintain a journal, state officials strongly recommend that, each time a Notary performs a notarial act, he or she record the signer's name, the method of identification, the date of notarization, and any additional pertinent information in a recordbook.

Of course, the National Notary Association and many Notary-regulating officials across the nation strongly endorse the policy of keeping a journal of all notarial acts as protection for both the public and the Notary.

Purpose. Prudent Notaries keep detailed and accurate journals of their notarial acts for many reasons:

- Keeping records is a businesslike practice that every conscientious businessperson and public official should engage in. Not keeping records of important transactions, whether private or public, is risky.

- A Notary's recordbook protects the public's rights to valuable property and to due process by providing documentary evidence in the event a document is lost or altered or if a transaction is later challenged.

- In the event of a civil lawsuit alleging that the Notary's negligence or misconduct caused the plaintiff serious financial harm, a detailed journal of notarial acts can protect the Notary by showing that reasonable care was used to identify a signer. It would be difficult to contend that the Notary did not bother to identify a signer if the Notary's journal contained a detailed description of the ID cards that the signer presented.

- Since civil lawsuits arising from a contested notarial act typically take place three to six years after the act occurs, the Notary normally cannot accurately testify in court about the particulars of a notarization without a journal to aid the Notary's memory.

- Journals of notarial acts prevent or abort baseless lawsuits by showing that a Notary did use reasonable care or that a transaction did occur as recorded. Journal thumbprints and signatures are especially effective in defeating such groundless suits.

- Requiring each document signer to leave a signature, or even a thumbprint, in the Notary's journal both deters attempted forgeries and provides strong evidence for a conviction should a forgery occur.

Journal Entries. The Notary's journal should contain the following information for each notarial act performed:

1) The date, time of day, and type of notarization (e.g., jurat, acknowledgment, etc.).

2) The type (or title) of document notarized (e.g., Deed of Trust, Affidavit of Support, etc.), including the number of pages and the date of the document.

3) The printed name and address and the signature of each person whose signature is notarized, including the signature of any subscribing witness; the signature, printed name and address of any credible witness; and the signature, printed name, and address of any witness to a signature by mark or to a signing on behalf of a person physically unable to sign.

4) A statement as to how the signer's identity was confirmed. If the signer was identified by personal knowledge, the

journal entry should read "personal knowledge." If the signer was identified by identification document, the journal entry should contain a description of the ID card accepted, including the type of ID, the government agency issuing the ID, the serial or identifying number of the ID, and its date of issuance or expiration. If the signer was identified by credible identifying witness, the journal entry should contain the signature, name, and address of each witness.

5) The fee, if any, charged for the notarization.

Document Dates. If the document has a specific date on it, the Notary should record that date in the journal of notarial acts. Often the only date on a document is the date of the signature that is being notarized. If the signature is undated, however, the document may have no date on it at all. In that case, the Notary should record "no date" or "undated" in the journal.

For acknowledgments, the date the document was signed must either precede or be the same as the date of the notarization; it may not follow it. For a jurat, the date the document was signed and the date of the notarization must be the same.

A document whose signature is dated after the date on its notarial certificate risks rejection by a recorder, who may question how the document could have been notarized before it was signed.

Journal Signature. Perhaps the most important additional entry to obtain is the signer's signature. A journal signature protects the Notary against claims that a signer did not appear and is a deterrent to forgery, because it provides evidence of the signer's identity and appearance before the Notary.

To check for possible forgery, the Notary should compare the signature that the person leaves in the journal of notarial acts with the signatures on the document and on the IDs. The signatures should be at least reasonably similar.

The Notary also should observe the signing of the journal. If the signer appears to be laboring over the journal signature, this may be an indication of forgery in progress.

Since a journal signature is not required by law, the Notary may not refuse to notarize if the signer declines to leave one.

Journal Thumbprint. Many Notaries are asking document signers to leave a thumbprint in the journal. The journal thumbprint protects the Notary against claims that a signer did not appear and is a strong deterrent to forgery, because it represents absolute proof of the signer's identity and appearance before the Notary.

Provided the signer is willing, nothing prevents a Notary from asking for a thumbprint for every notarial act. Since a thumbprint is not required by law, however, the Notary may not refuse to notarize if the signer declines to leave one.

Additional Entries. Notaries may include additional information in the journal that is pertinent to a given notarization. Many Notaries, for example, enter the telephone number of all signers and witnesses. A description of the document signer's demeanor (e.g., "The signer appeared to be nervous.") or notations about the identity of other persons who were present for the notarization may also be pertinent.

One important entry to include is the signer's representative capacity — whether the signer is acting as attorney in fact, trustee, guardian, corporate officer or in another capacity — if not signing on his or her own behalf.

Complete Entry Before Certificate. The Notary should record the journal entry before filling out the Notary certificate on a document to prevent the signer from leaving with the notarized document before vital information is entered in the journal.

Inspection and Copying of Journal Entries. A Notary's official journal is a public record. Accordingly, any member of the public may ask to see a journal entry and/or for a photocopy of a journal entry.

Members of the public should not, however, be given free access to the Notary's journal, which contains sensitive personal information. Instead, the National Notary Association recommends that the Notary ask for a written request, specifying the month and year of a particular notarization, the type of document, and the names of the signers. The written request should then be kept with the journal as a part of the Notary's records.

Once the Notary has located the entry in question, the Notary may allow the person making the request to inspect the specified entry or may provide that person with a photocopy of that entry. The Notary should cover adjacent journal entries with a blank piece of paper before allowing the inspection or making the photocopy.

MINNESOTA NOTARY LAW PRIMER

The National Notary Association discourages "fishing expeditions" through the Notary journal by persons who are not able to be specific about the entry sought.

<u>Certified Copy of Journal Record</u>. If a signer or member of the public presenting the written request requests the Notary to certify the photocopy of the journal entry, the National Notary Association recommends that the Notary complete, sign and affix the Notary's official stamp to the following certificate wording and attach it to the photocopy:

State of Minnesota
County of _____

On this _____ day of _____ (month), _____ (year), I, _____ (name of Notary Public), the undersigned Notary Public, hereby declare that the attached reproduction of a Notary journal entry involving _____ _____ (describe document, noting date and signer[s]) is a true and correct photocopy made from a page in my Notary journal.

_____
(Signature of notarial officer)

Title (and Rank) _____ (Stamp)

My commission expires: _____

<u>Journal Security</u>. A Notary should never surrender control of his or her journal to anyone, unless expressly subpoenaed by a court order. The journal is the personal property of the Notary. Even when an employer has paid for the Notary's journal and stamp, they go with the Notary upon termination of employment; no person but the Notary may properly possess and use these official adjuncts of office (MS 359.03[1]).

When the journal is not in use, the Notary should keep it secure and accessible only to the Notary. If the journal is lost or stolen, the Notary should contact the Secretary of State (website, "Notary Commission Guide").

<u>Journal Exempt from Execution</u>. Since the journal of notarial acts is the Notary's personal property, the journal is also exempt from execution. This means that a private party or creditor cannot

attach the journal in a judgment to satisfy a debt owed by the Notary (MS 359.03[1]).

Disposition of Journal. Minnesota statute does not provide rules for the disposition of journals at the end of the Notary's term or career. The National Notary Association recommends that Notaries should safely store all completed journals during their careers and archive these records for at least 10 years from the date of the last entry recorded in the journal.

Notary Certificate

Requirement. In notarizing any document, a Minnesota Notary must complete a Notary certificate (MS 358.47[a]). The certificate is wording that indicates exactly what the Notary has certified (MS 358.47[c]). The Notary certificate may be either preprinted on the document itself or appear on an attachment to it (often referred to as a loose Notary certificate). The Notary certificate must be in English and be either physically or electronically signed and dated by the Notary in a manner that attributes the signature to that particular Notary (MS 358.47[a],[b]).

Required Certificate Elements. The law specifies that the following elements must be included in each certificate (MS 358.47[a]):

- The date of notarization

- The jurisdiction or venue indicating where the notarization is being performed

"State of Minnesota, County of _____," is the typical venue wording, with the county name inserted in the blank. The letters "SS." or "SCT." sometimes appear after the venue; they are an abbreviation of the traditional Latin word *scilicet*, meaning "in particular" or "namely."

- The official signature of the Notary exactly as the name appears on the Notary's official stamp and on his or her commission

A signature stamp may not be used. Minnesota law specifically states that a Notary's signature must be original for documents affecting real estate or for documents that will be recorded (MS 507.24).

- The typed, printed or stamped name of the Notary

The official inking stamp containing the Notary's commission name satisfies the statutory requirement that the Notary's name be affixed to every Notary certificate. (See "Notary Stamp," pages 35–38.)

- The title of the notarial officer performing the notarization (e.g. "Notary Public")

- The official stamp of the Notary

On many certificates, the letters "L.S." appear, indicating where the stamp is to be located. These letters abbreviate the Latin term *locus sigilli*, meaning "place of the seal." The impression made by the inking stamp should be placed near — but not over — the letters so that wording imprinted by the stamp will not be obscured.

- If the notarizing officer is also a commissioned officer on active duty in the U.S. military service, his or her rank

Other Certificate Elements. In addition, Notary certificates typically contain the following elements:

- A statement of particulars, indicating what the Notary has attested to

For example, an acknowledgment certificate would include such wording as: "On _____ (date) before me, _____ (name of Notary), personally appeared _____ (name of signer), personally known to me (or proved to me on the basis of satisfactory evidence) to be the person(s)..." A jurat certificate would include such wording as: "Subscribed and sworn to (or affirmed) before me this _____ (date) by _____ (name of signer)."

- A testimonium clause

Typical testimonium clause wording reads: "Witness my hand and official seal, this the _____ day of _____ (month), _____ (year)." ("Hand" means signature.) In this sentence, the Notary formally attests to the truthfulness of the facts in the Notary certificate. This clause may be omitted if the date is included in the statement of particulars.

Signature Form for Ex Officio Notaries. Ex officio Notaries must sign certificates with their official signatures with the form of the signature appearing as follows (MS 358.15):

- Members of the legislature still residing in the district where they were elected: "[Name of officer], Representative (or Senator), _____ District, Minnesota, ex officio notary public. My term expires January 1, _____."

- Clerks or recorders of towns and cities: "Name of officer], [official title], _____ County, Minnesota, ex officio notary public. My term expires _____" (or, where applicable, "My term is indeterminate")."

- Court commissioners, county recorders and county auditors, and their several deputies, and county commissioners, all within their respective counties: "[Name of officer], [official title], _____ County, Minnesota, ex officio notary public. My term expires _____" (or, where applicable, "My term is indeterminate")."

- Peace officers licensed to administer oaths and affirmations: "[Name of officer], Peace Officer, License Number _____, _____ County, Minnesota. My license expires June 30, _____."

Form of Certificates. Minnesota law specifies that the form of a Notary certificate is sufficient if it is in English and meets the following criteria (MS 358.47[b]):

- The certificate is one of the statutory short forms provided in section 358.48 of the Minnesota Statutes.

- The certificate is in a form otherwise prescribed by Minnesota law.

- The certificate is in a form prescribed by the laws or regulations of the jurisdiction where the notarial act was performed.

- The certificate sufficiently sets forth the actions of the Notary officer to meet the requirements for the notarial act.

Completing the Certificate. When filling in the blanks in the notarial certificate, Notaries should either type or print neatly in dark ink.

Notaries also must pay attention to spaces on the notarial certificate that indicate the number and gender of the document signers, as well as how they were identified — for example, leave the plural "(s)" untouched or cross it out, as appropriate.

Correcting a Certificate. When filling out the certificate, the Notary needs to make sure any preprinted information is accurate. For example, the venue — the state and county in which the notarial act is taking place — may have been filled in prior to the notarization. If the preprinted venue is incorrect, the Notary must line through the incorrect state and/or county, write in the proper site of the notarization, and initial and date the change.

Loose Certificates. When certificate wording is not preprinted on the document for the Notary to fill out, a "loose" certificate may be attached. Normally, this form is stapled to the document's left margin following the signature page.

To prevent a loose certificate from being removed and fraudulently placed on another document, there are precautions a Notary can take. The Notary can write a brief description of the document on the certificate, e.g., "This certificate is attached to a _____ (title or type of document), dated _____, of _____ (number) pages, also signed by _____ (name[s] of other signer[s])." The Notary also can note on the document that a certificate is attached, e.g., "See attached Notary certificate, dated _____ (date) and certifying the signature(s) of _____ (name[s] of signer[s])."

While fraud-deterrent steps such as these can make it much more difficult for a loose certificate to be removed and misused, there is no absolute protection against its removal and misuse. Notaries must absolutely ensure that, while a certificate remains in their control, it is attached only to its intended document.

Do Not Pre-Sign or Pre-Stamp Certificates. A Notary should *never* sign and/or stamp certificates ahead of time or permit other persons to attach loose Notary certificates to documents. Nor should the Notary send an unattached, signed and stamped loose certificate through the mail — whether blank or complete — even if requested to do so by a signer who previously appeared before the Notary. These actions are dangerous because they may facilitate fraud or forgery, and they could subject the Notary to lawsuits to recover damages resulting from the Notary's negligence or misconduct.

Selecting Certificates. It is not the role of the Notary to decide what type of certificate — and thus what type of notarization — a document needs. As ministerial officials, Notaries generally follow instructions and complete forms that have been provided for them; they do not issue instructions or decide which forms are appropriate in a given case.

If a document is presented to a Notary without certificate wording and if the signer does not know what type of notarial act is appropriate, the signer should be asked to find out what kind of notarization and certificate are needed. Usually, the agency that issued the document or the one that will be accepting the document can provide this information. A Notary who selects certificates may be engaging in the unauthorized practice of law.

False Certificate. A Notary who knowingly completes a false Notary certificate is guilty of a misdemeanor and subject to a fine of up to $1,000, imprisonment for up to three months or both; or, if done with intent to injure or defraud, to a fine of up to $5,000, imprisonment for up to three years or both. For example, a Notary would be completing a false certificate if he or she signed and stamped an acknowledgment certificate indicating that a signer personally appeared when the signer actually did not (MS 609.65).

Blank Certificate. A Notary should never issue a Notary certificate that contains blank spaces or is otherwise incomplete. This is an unwise and dangerous practice, analogous to writing a blank check.

Notary Stamp

Requirement. All Minnesota Notaries must obtain an official Notary stamp with which to authenticate their notarial acts (MS 359.03[1]). Notaries must affix a photographically reproducible image or impression of their official stamp near their signatures on the certificate portion of every document notarized (MS 358.47[a] and 359.03[3]). Since only a stamp "which legibly reproduces under photographic methods" is allowed, a Notary's official stamp must be an inked rubber stamp. A metal embosser may be used only as an adjunct. (See "Embosser as Adjunct Device," see page 37.)

Stamp Format. Minnesota law specifies that the Notary's official stamp must be a rectangle no larger than three quarters of an inch by two and one-half inches and must have a serrated or milled-edge border (MS 359.03[3]).

Stamp Components. The impression or image of the Notary's official stamp must clearly show the following information (MS 359.03[3]):

- The Minnesota State Seal

- The name of the Notary exactly as it appears on the commission certificate or the name of the ex officio Notary

- The words "Notary Public" or, in the case of ex officio Notaries, "Notarial Officer"

- The words "My commission expires ..." followed by the Notary's commission expiration date or, where applicable, the words "My term is indeterminate"

Requirement for Ex Officio Notaries. All ex officio Notaries must obtain an official Notary stamp that meets the same criteria as the stamps of other Minnesota Notaries and must use their stamps to authenticate their official acts in the same fashion as Notaries who have been granted a commission (MS 358.15[b]).

County auditors, county recorders, the deputies of county auditors and recorders, and the clerks or recorders of towns or cities may authenticate their notarial acts without using the official stamp for 90 days after initially assuming the office, for 90 days after the effective date above, or until the officer acquires an official stamp, whichever is earlier (MS 358.15[c]).

Stamp Considered a Seal in Evidence. The official notarial stamp is considered a "seal" for the purposes of admission of a document in court (MS 359.03[2][b]).

Embosser as Adjunct Device. Notaries may use a metal embossing seal which crimps its impression onto a paper surface and aids distinguishing photocopies from originals in addition to the state required inked Notary stamp. However, the embosser may not be used alone as the Notary's official stamp.

If an embosser is used, it must include the following information:

- The Minnesota State Seal

- The words "Notarial Seal"

Placement of Stamp Impression. The Notary's official stamp impression should be placed near the Notary's signature on the Notary certificate. It must be easily readable and should not be placed over signatures or any printed matter on the document. An illegible or improperly placed stamp may result in the rejection of the document by a recorder.

If there is no room for the stamp, the Notary may have no choice but to complete and attach a loose certificate that duplicates the notarial wording on the document.

L.S. The letters "L.S." — from the Latin words *locus sigilli*, meaning "location of the seal" — appear on many Notary certificates to indicate where the Notary stamp should be placed. Only an embossing seal should be placed over these letters. The impression made with the inking stamp should be placed near but not over the letters.

Illegible Stamp. If an initial stamp impression is unreadable and there is ample room on the document, another impression can be affixed nearby. The illegibility of the first impression will indicate why a second stamp impression was necessary. The Notary should then record in the journal that a second impression was applied.

A Notary should never attempt to fix an imperfect stamp impression with pen, ink or correction fluid. This may be viewed as evidence of tampering and cause the document to be rejected by a receiving agency.

Stamp Security. A Notary should never surrender control of his or her stamp to anyone. The official stamp is the personal property of the Notary. Even when an employer has paid for the Notary's journal and stamp, they go with the Notary upon termination of employment; no person but the Notary may properly possess and use these official adjuncts of office (MS 359.03[1]).

When the stamp is not in use, the Notary should keep it secure and accessible only to the Notary. If the stamp is lost or stolen, the Notary should contact the Secretary of State (website, "Notary Commission Guide").

Stamp Exempt from Execution. Since the official stamp is the Notary's personal property, the stamp is also exempt from execution. This means that a private party or creditor cannot attach the stamp in a judgment to satisfy a debt owed by the Notary (MS 359.03[1]).

Disposition of Stamp. Minnesota statute does not provide rules for the disposition of official stamps at the end of the Notary's term or career. The National Notary Association recommends that Notaries should promptly destroy official stamps at the end of each commission term so they cannot be used.

A Notary whose commission has been revoked must deliver his or her official stamp to the Commissioner of Commerce (MS 359.12).

Fees for Notary Services

Maximum Fees. Notaries may charge the following maximum fees for performing notarial acts (MS 357.17): [Additional acts (copy certification, signature witnessing) are listed under "Authorized Acts," pages 8–9.]

- Acknowledgments — $5. For taking an acknowledgment, the legal fee allowed other officers for like services may be charged, typically $5 for each signature. For example, for notarizing a single document with the signatures of three different persons appearing before the Notary, a maximum of $15 may be charged.

- Verifications Upon Oath or Affirmation — $5. For executing a verification on an affidavit, including the administration of the oath or affirmation, the fee is not to exceed $5 per folio, plus $1 per folio for copies.

- Oaths and Affirmations — $5. For administering an oath or affirmation, with or without the completion of a jurat, the fee is not to exceed $5 per oath.

- Protests — $5. For executing a protest, with copy, the fee is not to exceed $5. For making and serving every notice of nonpayment or nonacceptance, with copy, $5 may be charged.

Option Not to Charge. Notaries are not required to charge for their Notary services, and they may charge any fee less than the maximum.

Certain Ex Officio Notaries May Not Charge. Ex officio Notaries who are members of the legislature may not charge a fee for notarizing (MS 358.15[a][1]).

Overcharging Prohibited. A Notary who charges more than the legally prescribed fees may face any of the penalties at the disposal of the Commissioner of Commerce (MS 359.12). (See "Administrative Penalties," pages 55–56.)

Discrimination. Setting the fee for a notarial act based upon the attributes (e.g., religion, race, status as a client or non-client) of the signer or as a result of the Notary's personal bias, is improper for the public servant Notary. Notaries must charge all signers fairly and even-handedly.

Travel Fees. Charges for travel by a Notary are not specified by law. Such fees are allowed only if the Notary and signer agree beforehand on the amount to be charged. The Notary must tell the signer that a travel fee is not stated in the law and is separate from the Notary fees.

Unauthorized Practice of Law

Do Not Assist Others with Legal Matters. A nonattorney Notary may not give legal advice or accept fees for legal advice. As a ministerial officer, the nonattorney Notary is generally not permitted to assist other persons in drafting, preparing, selecting, completing or understanding a document or transaction. Notaries who overstep their authority by advising others on legal matters may be prosecuted for the unauthorized practice of law (MS 481.02).

The Notary should not fill in blank spaces in the text of a document for other persons, tell others what documents they need nor how to draft them or advise others about the legal sufficiency of a document — and especially not for a fee. A Notary, of course, may fill in the blanks on the portion of any document containing the Notary certificate. And a Notary, as a private individual, may prepare legal documents that he or she is personally a party to, but the Notary may not then notarize his or her signature on these same documents.

Exceptions. Nonattorney Notaries who are specially trained or licensed in a particular field (e.g., real estate, insurance or escrow) may advise others about documents in that field, but in no other. In addition, a specialized legal assistant who has a specialty license issued by the Supreme Court before July 1, 1995 may deliver legal services (MS 481.02[3][14]).

Disqualifying Interest

Impartiality. Notaries are appointed by the state to be impartial, disinterested witnesses whose screening duties help ensure the integrity of important legal and commercial transactions. Lack of impartiality by a Notary throws doubt on the integrity and lawfulness of any transaction.

Notarizing Own Signature Prohibited. A Notary must never notarize his or her own signature or administer his or her own oath or affirmation (MS 359.085[7]).

Financial or Beneficial Interest. A Notary should not perform any notarization related to a transaction in which that Notary has a direct financial or beneficial interest. A financial or beneficial interest exists when the Notary is individually named as a principal or beneficiary in a financial transaction or when the Notary receives an advantage, right, privilege, property, fee or any other benefit valued in excess of the fee prescribed by law.

Disqualified if Health Care Agent. A Notary appointed as a health care agent or alternate health care agent in a health care power of attorney may not notarize the health care directive that contains the health care power of attorney (MS 145C.03[3]).

Relatives. The National Notary Association strongly advises against notarizing for persons related by blood or marriage because of the likelihood of a financial or beneficial interest, whether large or small. Often, a Notary will have a clear-cut disqualifying financial or beneficial interest in notarizing for a close friend or relative, especially for the Notary's spouse. If the Notary's spouse, for example, purchases a home in which the couple will live, then the Notary should not notarize the deed for the purchase.

It is often difficult for a Notary to retain impartiality with a close relative. A person may be entitled to counsel a brother, spouse or other relative to sign or not to sign an important document, but such counseling is entirely inappropriate for an individual serving as the Notary in the transaction.

Employers. A Notary who notarizes for an employer that receives a benefit from a transaction is not considered to have a disqualifying interest unless he or she receives consideration other than a salary and the statutory fee for notarization.

Corporate Officers. A Notary who is an officer, director or stockholder of a corporation may notarize for that corporation (MS 358.25).

Refusal of Services

Discrimination. Notaries should honor all lawful and reasonable requests to notarize. A person's race, age, gender, religion, nationality, ethnicity, lifestyle or political viewpoint is never legitimate cause for refusing to perform a notarial act.

Noncustomers. Notary-employees may refuse to notarize for noncustomers if their employer has limited the services of Notary-employees to business-related notarizations during hours of employment and has excluded services to the public.

Accommodation of Physical Limitations

Signature by Mark. A person who cannot sign his or her name because of illiteracy or a physical disability generally may instead use a mark — an "X" for example — as a legal signature. In the absence of a specific statute or official rule, the National Notary Association recommends that two impartial witnesses view the affixing of the mark. Both witnesses should sign the document (e.g., "John Q. Smith, Witness") and the Notary's journal. One witness should clearly print the name of the principal near the mark. Because a mark is generally considered a signature under law, as long as it is properly witnessed, no special Notary certificate is required for persons signing by mark. A Notary should use a standard acknowledgment, jurat or signature witnessing certificate.

<u>Signature by Proxy</u>. If a prospective signer has a physical limitation that restricts his or her ability to sign by writing or making a mark, then the Notary may perform a notarial act for that person under the following circumstances (MS 359.091):

- The signature of the signer may be applied (or, in the case of an electronic signature, attached electronically) by another individual at the direction of the signer and in the presence of both the signer and the Notary. The signature may be applied by means of a rubber stamp facsimile of the signer's actual signature or mark, or by means of a written signature of the signer's name or mark made by another individual. Whatever the means used, it must be adopted for all purposes of signature by the signer with a physical limitation. The individual signing for the principal in this situation may not be the Notary.

- Beneath or near the signer's signature must appear the following words or words of substantially similar effect:

In the case of a paper record, "Signature written by (name of the individual directed by the signer to sign the signature at the direction and in the presence of (name of signer), on whose behalf the signature was written."

In the case of an electronic record, "Signature attached by (name of the individual directed by the signer to attach the signature) at the direction and in the presence of (name of signer), on whose behalf the signature was electronically attached."

<u>Nonverbal Communication Permitted</u>. If a prospective signer or other individual appearing before the Notary has a physical limitation that restricts his or her ability to communicate with the Notary either verbally or in writing, then the Notary may use signals or electronic or mechanical means to take an acknowledgment from, administer an oath or affirmation to, or otherwise communicate with that person (MS 359.091).

Notarizing for Minors

Under Age 18. Generally, persons must reach the age of majority before they can handle their own legal affairs and sign documents for themselves. In Minnesota, the age of majority is 18. Normally, natural guardians (parents) or court-appointed guardians will sign on a minor's behalf. In certain cases, emancipated minors may serve as court witnesses, lawfully sign documents and have their signatures notarized.

Include Age Next to Signature. When notarizing for a minor, the Notary should ask the young signer to write his or her age next to the signature to alert any person relying upon the document that the signer is a minor. The Notary is not required to verify the minor signer's age.

Identification. The method for identifying a minor is the same as that for an adult. However, determining the identity of a minor can be a problem, because minors often do not possess reliable identification documents such as driver's licenses or passports. If the minor does not have a reliable ID, then the Notary must base identification on the Notary's personal knowledge of the minor's identity or the oath of a credible identifying witness. (See "Credible Identifying Witness," pages 25–26.)

Wills

Advice or Assistance Prohibited. Wills are highly sensitive documents, the format of which is dictated by strict laws. The slightest deviation from these laws can nullify a will. In some cases, holographic (handwritten) wills have actually been voided by notarization. Often, people attempt to draw up wills without benefit of legal counsel and then bring these homemade testaments to a Notary to have them "legalized," expecting the Notary to know how to proceed. In advising or assisting such persons, the Notary risks prosecution for the unauthorized practice of law; the Notary's ill-informed advice may do considerable damage to the affairs of the signer or others.

In Minnesota, a last will is not typically notarized, but signed by the testator in the presence of two witnesses (MS 524.02-502). A Minnesota Notary may notarize the signature on a will as long as a Notary certificate is provided for the Notary to fill out and the signer is not seeking advice from the Notary on how to proceed.

MINNESOTA NOTARY LAW PRIMER

Self-Proving Wills. A Minnesota Notary may notarize the signatures of the testator and witnesses on separate us at the time the will is executed or at some later date, making the will "self-proving." The advantage of making a will self-proving is that when the will is actually submitted to probate years later, the witnesses will not need to be summoned to attest to the proper execution of the will (MS 524.2-504).

Living Wills. Documents that are popularly called "living wills" may be notarized. These are not actually wills at all, but written statements of the signer's wishes concerning medical treatment in the event the person has an illness or injury and is unable to issue instructions on his or her own behalf.

Advertising

Non-English Advertising. Nonattorney Notaries who advertise their services in a foreign language, whether by radio, television, signs, pamphlets, newspapers or other written communication, except for a single desk plaque, must post a prescribed notice in English and the foreign language in which the ad appears.

If written, the notice must be of a conspicuous size, and must state, "I AM NOT AN ATTORNEY LICENSED TO PRACTICE LAW IN MINNESOTA, AND MAY NOT GIVE LEGAL ADVICE OR ACCEPT FEES FOR LEGAL ADVICE." If appearing on radio or television, the prescribed statement may be modified but must include substantially the same message.

A nonattorney Notary who fails to post the prescribed notice in a foreign-language advertisement is guilty of a misdemeanor (MS 359.062).

Foreign Languages

Foreign-Language Documents. Ideally, documents in foreign languages should be referred to Minnesota Notaries who read and write those languages. If not available in the general public, bilingual Notaries may often be found in foreign consulates in the larger cities.

Minnesota Notaries are not expressly prohibited from notarizing non-English documents. If a Notary notarizes a document that he or she cannot read, then the Notary certificate should be in English, or in a language the Notary can read.

However, there are difficulties to consider with these documents: blatant fraud might go undetected; the U.S. Notary stamp might be misinterpreted in another country; and determining the nature of the document for a journal entry might be difficult.

Foreign-Language Speakers. A Notary should notarize only for signers who speak the same language as the Notary. There should always be direct communication between the Notary and document signer, whether in English or any other language. The Notary should never rely upon an intermediary or interpreter to be assured that a signer is willing and aware, for this third party may have a motive for misrepresenting the circumstances to the Notary and/or to the signer.

Immigration Documents

Advice or Assistance Prohibited. Nonattorney Notaries may never advise others on the subject of immigration or help others prepare immigration documents — especially not for a fee. Notaries who offer immigration advice to others may be prosecuted for the unauthorized practice of law.

Notarizing Immigration Documents. Certain immigration documents accepted by the U.S. Citizenship and Immigration Services (USCIS) may be notarized. However, federal law does place certain restrictions on the Notary in the area of immigration. (See "Naturalization Certificates," page 45.)

Documents not issued by USCIS are often notarized and submitted in support of an immigration petition. These include translator's declarations, statements from employers and banks, and affidavits of relationship.

Naturalization Certificates. A Notary may only photocopy a certificate of naturalization for lawful purposes. The NNA recommends a Notary only certify a copy of the certificate if written directions are provided by a U.S. immigration authority.

Incomplete Documents

Do Not Notarize. Even though notarizing a document with blank spaces is not addressed in Minnesota law, it is a dangerous, unprofessional practice and a breach of common sense, similar to signing a blank check.

A fraudulent document could readily be created above a Notary's signed and stamped certificate on an otherwise blank paper. With documents containing blanks to be filled in by a person other than the signer after the notarization, there is a danger that the information inserted will be contrary to the wishes of the signer.

Blanks in a document should be filled in by the signer prior to notarization. If the blanks are inapplicable and intended to be left unfilled, the signer should line through each space or write "Not Applicable" or "N/A." The Notary may not, however, tell the signer what to write in the blanks. If the signer is unsure what to put, he or she should contact the document's issuer, its eventual recipient, or an attorney.

Photocopies & Faxes

Original Signature. A photocopy or fax may be notarized as long as the signature on it is original, meaning that the photocopy or fax must have been signed with pen and ink. Signatures on documents presented for notarization must always be signed with a handwritten, original signature. A photocopied or faxed signature may never be notarized.

Note that public recorders sometimes will not accept notarized photocopies or faxes, because the text of the document may be too faint to adequately reproduce in microfilming.

Military-Personnel Notarizations

May Notarize Worldwide. Certain U.S. military personnel may notarize anywhere in the world for (U.S. Code, Title 10, Section 1044[a]):

- Members of any of the armed forces.

- Other persons eligible for legal assistance under U.S. Code Title 10, Section 1044, or under Department of Defense regulations.

- Persons serving with, employed by, or accompanying the armed forces outside the United States and its territories.

- Other persons subject to the Uniform Code of Military Justice outside the United States.

Under statutory authority, the following persons are authorized to act as Notaries (U.S. Code, Title 10, Section 1044[b]):

- Civilian attorneys serving as legal assistance attorneys.

- Judge advocates, including reserve judge advocates when not in a duty status.

- All adjutants, assistant adjutants, and personnel adjutants, including reserve members when not in a duty status.

- All other members of the armed forces, including reserve members when not in a duty status, who are designated by regulations of the armed forces or by statute to have those powers.

- For the performance of notarial acts outside the United States only, all employees of a military department or of the Coast Guard who are designated by regulations of the Secretary concerned or by statute to have those powers.

Fee. Military-personnel Notaries may not charge or receive a fee for their services (U.S. Code, Title 10, Section 1044[c]).

Authentication. Authentication of a military-personnel notarization certificate is not required (U.S. Code, Title 10, Section 1044[d]).

Authentication

Purpose. Documents notarized in Minnesota and sent to other states or nations may be required to bear proof that the Notary's signature and stamp are genuine and that the Notary had authority to act at the time of notarization. This process of proving the genuineness of an official signature and stamp is called *authentication* or *legalization*.

Certificate. These authenticating certificates are known by different names: certificates of authority, certificates of capacity, certificates of authenticity, certificates of prothonotary, and "flags."

Procedure. In Minnesota, since the commission and signature of every Notary have been recorded with the local registrar or other Notary-regulating official in the county in which the Notary was appointed, such a county official or the Secretary of State can provide authentication of a Notary's signature and stamp in the form of a certificate attached to the notarized document (MS 359.061 and website, "Frequently Asked Questions").

If the authenticating certificate is issued by the county court administrator, then the fee is that prescribed by statute or court rule. If the certificate is issued by another Notary-regulating official, then the fee is $5 per certificate (MS 359.061).

<u>Documents Sent Out of the Country</u>. If the notarized document is destined for a country outside the United States, a "chain" authentication process may be necessary. Additional certificates of authority may have to be obtained from the U.S. Department of State in Washington, D.C., a foreign consulate in Washington, D.C., and a ministry of foreign affairs in the particular foreign nation.

Apostilles. More than 100 nations, including the United States, participate in a treaty that streamlines the authentication of notarized documents sent between any two of the participating nations. This treaty is called *The Hague Convention Abolishing the Requirement of Legalization for Foreign Public Documents*, hereafter simply called The Hague Convention. The Hague Convention permits one-step verification of a Notary's authority through the use of a standard certificate called an *apostille* (French for "notation"). When the Minnesota Secretary of State or his or her agent issues an *apostille* for a notarized document bound for a country that participates in The Hague Convention, that certificate is the only proof of notarial authority required.

<u>Authentications</u>. For documents bound for a country that is not a participant in The Hague Convention, the Minnesota Secretary of State or his or her agent issues an authenticating "certificate of office." Certificates of office, unlike *apostilles*, vary in format from country to country and from jurisdiction to jurisdiction. Some countries accept a document bearing a single authentication certificate, while other countries require the document to be authenticated through a lengthier chain-certification process (website, "Authentications and Apostilles").

<u>Chain Certifications</u>. The chain-certification process can be quite complicated and time-consuming. It requires the attachment to the document of several different authenticating certificates. Each certificate in the chain-certification process validates the authenticity of the preceding certificate. Additional certificates of

authority may need to be requested from the U.S. Department of State in Washington, D.C., a foreign consulate in Washington, D.C. and a ministry of foreign affairs in the particular foreign nation (website, "Authentications and Apostilles").

Requesting an *Apostille* or Authentication. It is not the Notary's responsibility to pick up or pay for an authenticating certificate. The person who requires an *apostille* or authentication may obtain either certificate in person or by mail at the address below. The office is open Monday – Friday from 8 a.m. to 4 p.m., excluding holidays. To obtain a certificate by mail, the person should send a written request (including the country to which the document will be sent) with the original notarized document, a self-addressed, stamped envelope, or pre-addressed, prepaid air bill and a $5 check or money order for each authentication certificate made payable to "MN Secretary of State" (website, "Authentications and Apostilles").

> Minnesota Secretary of State – Certification
> Retirement Systems Building of Minnesota
> 60 Empire Drive, Suite 100
> Saint Paul, MN 55103-2141

Notarial Acts From Other U.S. Jurisdictions Received in State. If a document is notarized or a notarial act is performed in another state or jurisdiction of the United States by a Notary, by a judge, clerk, or deputy clerk of a court or by any other person authorized to perform notarial acts in that state or jurisdiction, no authentication is required: the notarization has the same effect as one performed by a Minnesota notarial officer. The signature and title of the person performing the notarial act are *prima facie* evidence that the signature is genuine and that the person holds the title as a notarizing officer (MS 358.44).

Notarial Acts Under U.S. Authority Received in State. If a document is notarized or a notarial act is performed anywhere by a designated officer under federal authority, including by a judge, clerk or deputy clerk of a court, by a commissioned officer in active military service of the United States, by a consular officer or officer of the foreign service or by any other person authorized under federal law to perform notarial acts, no authentication is required: the notarization has the same effect as one performed by a Minnesota notarial officer. The signature and title of the person performing the notarial act are *prima facie* evidence that the signature is genuine and that the person holds the title as a notarizing officer (MS 358.45).

Notarial Acts from Abroad Received in State. If a document is notarized or a notarial act is performed within and under authority of a foreign nation or its constituent units, or a multinational or international organization by a Notary Public, by a judge, clerk or deputy clerk of a court or by any other person authorized by the jurisdiction to perform notarial acts, the notarization or notarial act has the same effect as one performed by a Minnesota notarial officer.

An *apostille* attached to the notarized document originating from a foreign nation or entity party to The Hague Convention conclusively establishes that the signature of the notarial officer is genuine and that the officer holds the indicated office.

A certification by a foreign service or consular officer of the U.S. stationed in the nation under which the notarial act was performed, or by a foreign service or consular officer of that nation stationed in the U.S. conclusively establishes any matter relating to the authenticity or validity of the notarial act (MS 358.46).

Other means of conclusively establishing the signature and title of a person performing a notarial act from abroad and received in Minnesota are the presence of an official stamp or seal or the listing of the title of office and authority to perform notarial acts in a digest of foreign law or in a list customarily used as a source of that information (MS 358.46[d], [e] and [f]).

ELECTRONIC NOTARIZATION

Statutory Authority

Electronic commerce produces a need for Notaries to witness electronic transactions, just as Notaries have witnessed paper transactions for centuries. While the tools for creating and signing documents may be different, the impartial witnessing services of a Notary remain the same and are as important as ever.

UETA. Minnesota enacted the Uniform Electronic Transactions Act, or UETA, in 2001. UETA is a uniform law governing electronic transactions. UETA has been adopted by nearly every state and the District of Columbia.

NOTARY LAWS EXPLAINED

Electronic Transactions Legal. The UETA recognizes that electronic documents and electronic signatures may be used with the same legal effect as paper documents and pen-and-ink signatures. Significantly, UETA states that a transaction cannot be denied legal effect or rejected because it is in electronic form or because electronic means — such as computer hardware, software and electronic signatures — were used in its creation and execution. Further, the UETA says that if a law requires a transaction to be in writing, an electronic document satisfies the law (MS 325L.07).

Electronic Notarizations Legal. The UETA authorizes Notaries to use electronic signatures in signing electronic documents if all other information required to be included — for example, the Notary's typed name, the title "Notary Public" and commission expiration date — is attached to or logically associated with the electronic record or signature (MS 325L.11). (See "Electronic Notary Stamp," pages 53–54.)

Technological Neutrality. An important principle of the UETA is "technological neutrality." The UETA does not specify or endorse a particular technology for creating, signing, transmitting and storing electronic records nor for affixing electronic signatures. Instead, the parties involved in a transaction simply must agree upon the technology used to sign a document electronically.

Electronic Signatures. A paper document is signed with pen and ink, but an electronic document — one that is created, sent, received or stored by electronic means (MS 325L.02 and 358.41) — may be "signed" and authenticated with an electronic signature using any available technology. Minnesota law defines an electronic signature as an electronic sound, symbol or process executed by a person with the intent to sign an electronic document (MS 325L.02 and 358.41). Examples of electronic signatures may include:

- a typed name, such as one on the signature line of an electronic document or at the bottom of an email;

- a "click wrap" signature created when a signer clicks an "I accept" or "Click to Sign" button in a software application or on a website, such as when purchasing items online with a credit card;

51

- a scanned image of a handwritten signature pasted into an electronic document;

- a handwritten signature made by using an electronic signature pad or device;

- a voice print, based on the unique physical configuration of the speaker's mouth and throat, which expresses the vocal sample as a mathematical formula;

- a voice message left by telephone;

- a Personal Identification Number (PIN), such as those used at a bank ATM;

- a telephone prompt or code entered using the dial pad of a touch-tone phone;

- a digital signature affixed by applying cryptographic methods.

Intent. One of the most important legal considerations of any electronic signature is intent. Regardless of the actual technology used to create an e-signature, the party using the technology must adopt it with the intent to sign the electronic document (MS 325L.02[h] and 358.41[6]).

Attribution and Security Procedure. Another critically important legal consideration of any electronic signature is attribution. The term attribution describes the process of determining that a signature is the act of a given person (MS 325L.09[a]). Knowing just who actually signed an electronic document is a fundamental concern. The UETA allows parties executing an electronic transaction to use a "security procedure" to determine the person to which the electronic signature is attributable (MS 325L.09[a]) and to detect changes or errors in the signed record (MS 325L.02[n]). A security procedure can use technological means — including algorithms or other codes, identifying words or numbers, encryption, callback or other acknowledgment procedures and the like — to prove that a signature is the act of a given person and that the content of the document has not been changed since it was signed (MS 325L.02[n]). In addition, a security procedure can use non-technological means. As an "acknowledgment procedure," a notarial act qualifies as a security procedure for proving attribution of an electronic signature.

Electronic Recording. In 2008, Minnesota enacted the Uniform Real Property Electronic Recording Act (URPERA), permitting county recorders to accept electronic real property documents for recordation. The URPERA permits Notaries to sign electronic real property records using an electronic signature without an imprint of a physical or electronic image of a Notary's official stamp (MS 507.0943[c]).

Physical Presence Required. Notaries should not notarize the physical or electronic signature of any signer who is not in the Notary's presence at the time of notarization (website, "Notary Commission Guide").

Certificate for Electronic Record. A notarial act executed by electronic means must be evidenced by a certificate that has been electronically signed by the Notary in a manner that attributes the signature to that particular Notary. The certificate also must include the date and venue of the notarization and the Notary's official electronic stamp, and the Notary's name as it appears in both the certificate and the stamp must be identical to the name that appears on the Notary's commission. If the Notary is an officer in the U.S. military, the certificate also must include his or her rank (MS 358.47[a]).

Electronic Notary Stamp. Notaries do not need to use a physical stamp or affix an electronic image of the physical stamp when notarizing electronic documents, particularly electronic real property documents (MS 507.0943[c]). However, as indicated above, electronic notarizations must include a Notary certificate that contains the Notary's electronic Notary stamp.

A Minnesota Notary's electronic stamp must contain the same information as the Notary's physical stamp: the Minnesota State Seal; the Notary's name exactly as it appears on the commission certificate or the name of the ex officio Notary; the words "Notary Public" or, in the case of ex officio Notaries, "Notarial Officer;" and the words "My commission expires ..." followed by the Notary's commission expiration date or, where applicable, the words "My commission is indeterminate" (MS 359.03[3]). The information must be logically and securely affixed to or associated with the electronic record being notarized (MS 359.03[4]).

Registration as Electronic Notary

Required. Before performing electronic notarial acts, a Notary Public must register with the Secretary of State. An application for e-notarization authorization is available on the Secretary of State's website. Upon registration with the Secretary of State, the Notary will be issued an "e-notarization authorization" (MS 359.01[5]).

Electronic Signature by Proxy. The provisions related to accepting a signature made by a person who is directed by the document signer to sign apply in cases when an electronic signature is used. (See "Accommodation of Physical Limitations," pages 41–42.)

MISCONDUCT, FINES AND PENALTIES

Illegal and Improper Acts

Failing to Discharge Duty. A Notary who dishonestly or unfaithfully discharges his or her duties as a Notary may face any of the penalties at the disposal of the Commissioner of Commerce (MS 359.12). (See "Administrative Penalties," pages 55–56.)

Pleading Guilty or *Nolo Contendere* to Misdemeanor or Felony. A Notary who has pleaded guilty, with or without explicitly admitting guilt, or pleaded *nolo contendere* ("no contest") to a misdemeanor or felony is subject to any of the penalties at the disposal of the Commissioner of Commerce (MS 359.12). (See "Administrative Penalties," pages 55–56.)

Being Convicted of Misdemeanor or Felony. A Notary who has been convicted of a felony, gross misdemeanor or misdemeanor involving moral turpitude may face any of the penalties at the disposal of the Commissioner of Commerce (MS 359.12). (See "Administrative Penalties," pages 55–56.)

Completing False Certificate. A Notary who knowingly completes a false Notary certificate is guilty of a misdemeanor and subject to a fine of up to $1,000, or to imprisonment for up to three months, or both; or, if done with intent to injure or defraud, to a fine of up to $5,000, or to imprisonment for up to three years, or both (MS 609.65).

Unauthorized Practice of Law. Nonattorney Notaries are prohibited from assisting a signer in drafting, completing, selecting or understanding a document or transaction, or otherwise providing unauthorized legal advice (MS 481.02).

Notarizing Own Signature. A Notary may not notarize his or her own signature (MS 359.085[7]).

Notarizing as Health Care Agent. A Notary Public may not notarize a power of attorney for health care in which the Notary's name appears as a health care agent or alternate health care agent (MS 145C.03).

Improper Foreign-Language Advertising. A nonattorney Notary's failure to print or include the prescribed notice that one is not an attorney in a non-English advertisement is a misdemeanor (MS 359.062).

Overcharging. A Minnesota Notary may be removed from office and become ineligible to hold a future Notary commission for charging more than the maximum fees established by statute (MS 359.12).

Certifying Copies of Vital or Public Records. A Notary is not authorized to certify a copy of a document that is a vital or public record or is publicly recordable.

Notarizing after Commission Expires. It is a misdemeanor offense for a Minnesota Notary to perform notarial duties after the expiration of his or her term of office or when otherwise disqualified (MS 359.08).

Administrative Penalties

Grounds for Administrative Action. By order of the Commissioner of Commerce, a Notary's commission may be denied, suspended or revoked or a Notary may be censured for the following reasons (MS 45.027[7]):

- The order is in the public interest.

- The Notary has violated any law, rule or order related to the responsibilities under the Commissioner's oversight.

- The Notary has provided false, misleading or incomplete information to the Commissioner or has refused to allow a reasonable inspection of his or her records or premises.

- The Notary has engaged in an act or practice, whether or not the act or practice directly relates to the Notary's office, which demonstrates that the Notary is untrustworthy, financially irresponsible or otherwise incompetent or unqualified to act under the commission granted by the Commissioner.

Administrative Penalties. In addition to denying, suspending or revoking a Notary's commission, the Commissioner of Commerce may impose the following penalties on Notaries:

- If it appears to the Commissioner that a Notary has engaged or is about to engage in an act or practice that is a violation of a law, rule or order related to the duties and responsibilities entrusted to the Commissioner, then he or she may issue an order requiring the Notary to cease and desist (MS 45.027[5a]).

- The Commissioner may impose a civil penalty not to exceed $10,000 per violation upon a Notary who violates any law, rule or order related to the duties and responsibilities entrusted to the Commissioner unless a different penalty is specified (MS 45.027[6]).

- If a Notary's commission expires, is surrendered, withdrawn or terminated, or becomes ineffective for any other reason, then the Commissioner may, within two years after the commission was last effective, enter a revocation or suspension order as of the last date on which the commission was in effect or may impose a civil penalty (MS 45.027[11]).

- The Commissioner may issue a stop order denying effectiveness to or suspending or revoking any registration (MS 45.027[8]).

Removal from Office. Only the Governor, the district court or the Commissioner of Commerce may remove a Notary from office. If a Notary is removed from office by the Commissioner of Commerce, then the Notary must deliver his or her official Notary stamp to the Commissioner (MS 359.12).

Civil Lawsuit

Liability of Notaries. Besides administrative fines and suspension or revocation of the commission, and criminal penalties that include fines and/or imprisonment, a Notary guilty of misconduct or negligence may be subject to a civil lawsuit to recover damages.

As a ministerial official, a Minnesota Notary is liable for all damages caused by any intentional or unintentional misconduct or negligence.

Reasonable Care

Definition. Whenever a Notary performs a notarial act, he or she is expected to exercise what is known as "reasonable care." Reasonable care is the level of attentiveness and concern expected of a person of ordinary intelligence. The first rule of reasonable care is strict adherence to all laws governing Notaries and notarization. In situations not explicitly covered by statute, a Notary should make every effort to use common sense and behave in a responsible and ethical fashion, following the accepted standards of conduct and best practices for that situation.

Protection Against Liability. In the event of a civil suit, if a Notary can show to a judge or jury that he or she did everything expected of a reasonable person, the judge or jury is obligated by law to find the Notary not liable for damages. ■

Minnesota Laws Pertaining to Notaries Public

The pertinent parts of the Minnesota Statutes affecting Notaries and notarial acts are reprinted on the following pages.

MINNESOTA STATUTES
CHAPTER 357. FEES

357.021 Court Administrator of District Court; Fees.
***

Subd. 2. **Fee amounts.** The fees to be charged and collected by the court administrator shall be as follows:
***

(12) For recording notary commission, $20.

357.17 Notaries Public.
The maximum fees to be charged and collected by a notary public shall be as follows:

(1) for protest of nonpayment of note or bill of exchange or of nonacceptance of such bill; where protest is legally necessary, and copy thereof, $5;

(2) for every other protest and copy, $5;

(3) for making and serving every notice of nonpayment of note or nonacceptance of bill and copy thereof, $5;

(4) for any affidavit or paper for which provision is not made herein, $5 per folio, and $1 per folio for copies;

(5) for each oath administered, $5;

(6) for acknowledgments of deeds and for other services authorized by law, the legal fees allowed other officers for like services;

(7) for recording each instrument required by law to be recorded by the notary, $5 per folio.

EFFECTIVE DATE. This section is effective August 1, 2014, and applies to notary services provided on or after that date.

History: (7001) RL s 2705; 1983 c 175 s 1; 1986 c 444

CHAPTER 358. SEALS, OATHS, ACKNOWLEDGMENTS

358.01 Private seals abolished.
Private seals are abolished, and all written instruments formerly required by law to be sealed shall be equally effective for all purposes without a seal; but nothing herein shall apply to the use of corporate seals;
History: (6933) RL s 2652

358.02 Repealed, 1983 c 119 s 4

358.028 Legislators, official seals.
Every member of the legislature, while in office and residing in the district from which elected, may have an official notarial stamp, in the form provided in section 358.03, with which to authenticate official acts provided for in section 358.15.
History: 1955 c 72 s 1; 1986 c 444; 2010 c 380 s2

358.03 Form of official seals.
Upon every seal of a court or officer authorized or required to have a seal there shall be engraved the same device that is engraved on the seal of the state, and the name of the court or office in which it is to be used.
History: (6935) RL s 2654: 1947 c 199 s 1

358.04 Temporary seal, when used.
When any court of record is unprovided with a seal, the judge thereof may authorize the use of any temporary seal, or of any device by way of seal, until one is provided.
History: (6936) RL s 2655

358.05 Oath of office.
The oath of office to be taken by members and officers of either branch of the legislature shall be that prescribed by the Constitution of the state of Minnesota article IV, section 8. Every person elected or appointed to any other public office, including every official commissioner, or member of any public board or body, before transacting any of the business or exercising any privilege of such office, shall take and subscribe the oath defined in the Constitution of the state of Minnesota, article V, section 6.
History: (6963) RL s 2677: 1976 c 2 s 172

358.06 Trustees, referees.
Unless otherwise provided by law, every executor, administrator, guardian, trustee, referee, arbitrator, viewer, assessor, appraiser, and other person appointed by or made responsible to the court in any action or proceeding, before entering upon duties as such, shall take and subscribe the following oath:

"I, A.B., do swear that I will faithfully and justly perform all the duties of the office and trust which I now assume as (insert brief description of

MINNESOTA NOTARY LAW PRIMER

office), to the best of my ability. So help me God."

History: (6964) RL s 2678; 1986 c 444

358.07 Forms of oaths in various cases.

An oath substantially in the following forms shall be administered to the respective officers and persons hereinafter named:

(1) To grand jurors:

"You each do swear that you will diligently inquire, and true *presentment* make, of all public offenses committed within this county of which you have legal proof; the counsel of the state and of yourself and fellows you will keep secret; you will present no person through malice or ill-will, nor leave any unpresented through fear or favor, or the receipt or hope of reward, but will present things truly to the best of your understanding and according to law. So help you God."

(2) To petit jurors in civil actions:

"You each do swear that you will impartially try the issues in this case, and a true verdict give, according to law and the evidence given you in court; your own counsel and that of your fellows you will duly keep; you will say nothing to any person concerning the case, nor suffer any one to speak to you about it, and will keep your verdict secret until you deliver it in court. So help you God."

(3) To petit juries in criminal cases:

"You each do swear that, without respect of persons or favor of any person, you will well and truly try, and true deliverance make, between the state of Minnesota and the defendant, according to law and the evidence given you in court. So help you God."

(4) To officers attending grand juries:

"You do swear that, as officer of the grand jury, you will keep their counsel and that of the state, and not disclose anything relative to their proceedings. So help you God."

(5) To same in charge of petit juries:

"You do swear that you will keep this jury together, and, so far as may be, secluded, so long as they shall remain in your charge; will suffer no one to communicate with or overhear them while deliberating upon their verdict; and will not by word or sign disclose, except to the court alone, anything that may come to your knowledge concerning their action in this case until they are duly discharged."

(6) Same, in charge during recess:

"You do swear that you will keep together this jury until they return into court, and that in the meantime you will suffer no one to speak to them, nor speak to them yourself, concerning the cause on trial, or any matter relating thereto."

(7) To witnesses:

"You do swear that the evidence you shall give relative to the cause now under consideration shall be the whole truth, and nothing but the truth. So help you God."

(8) To interpreters:

"You do swear that you will truly and impartially interpret to this witness the oath about, to be administered to the witness, and the testimony the witness shall give relative to the cause now under consideration. So help you God."

(9) To attorneys:

"You do swear that you will support the constitution of the United States and that of the state of Minnesota, and will conduct yourself as an attorney and counselor at law in an upright and courteous manner, to the best of your learning and ability, with all good fidelity as well to the court as to the client, and that you will use no falsehood or deceit, nor delay any person's cause for lucre or malice. So help you God."

(10) To affiants:

"You do swear that the statements of this affidavit, by you subscribed, are true. So help you God."

History: (6965) RL s 2679; 1986 c 444

358.08 Affirmation in lieu of oath.

If any person of whom an oath is required shall claim religious scruples against taking the same, the word "swear" and the words "so help you God" may be omitted from the foregoing forms, and the word "affirm" and the words "and this you do under the penalties of perjury" shall be substituted therefor, respectively, and such person shall be considered, for all purposes, as having been duly sworn.

History: (6966) RL s 2680; 1986 c 444

358.09 By whom and how administered.

Any officer authorized by this chapter to take and certify acknowledgments may administer an oath, and, if the same be in writing, may certify the same under the officer's signature, and an official notarial stamp, in the following form: "Subscribed and sworn to before me this _____ day of _____ , _____" The mode of administering an oath commonly practiced in the place where it is taken shall be followed, including, in this state, the ceremony of uplifting the hand.

History: (6967) RL s 2681: 1986 c 444; 2010 c 380 s 3

358.10 Officials may administer, when.

All persons holding office under any law of this state, or under the charter or ordinances of any municipal corporation thereof, including judges and clerks of election, and all committee members, commissioners, trustees, referees, appraisers, assessors, and all others authorized or required by law to act or report upon any matter of fact, shall have power to administer such oaths as they may deem necessary to the proper discharge of their respective duties.

History: (6968) RL s 2682; 1986 c 444

358.11 Oaths, where filed.

Except as otherwise provided by law, the oath required to be taken and subscribed by any person shall be filed as follows:

(1) If that of an officer of the state, whether elective or appointive, with the secretary of state;

(2) If of a county officer, or an officer chosen within or for any county, with the county auditor;

(3) If of a city officer, with the clerk or recorder of the municipality;

(4) If of a town officer, with the town clerk;

(5) If of a school district officer, with the clerk of the district;

(6) If of a person appointed by, or made responsible to, a court in any action or proceeding therein, with the court administrator of such court;

(7) If that of a person appointed by any state, county, or other officer for a special service in connection with official duties, with such officer.

If the person taking such oath be also required to give bond, the oath shall be attached to or endorsed upon such bond and filed therewith, in lieu of other filing.

History: (6969) RL s 2683; 1973 c 123 art 5 s 7; 1986 c 444; 1Sp1986 c 3art 1 s 82

358.12 Repealed, 1973 c 116 s 10

358.13 Repealed, 1973 c 116 s 10

358.14 Married persons.

No separate examination of each spouse shall be required, but if husband and wife join in and acknowledge the execution of any instrument, they shall be described in the certificate of acknowledgment as husband and wife; and, if they acknowledge it before different officers, or before the same officer at different times, each shall be described in the certificate as the spouse of the other.

History: (6972) RL s 2686; 1987 c 49 s 10

358.15 Ex officio notary public.

(a) The following officers have the powers of a notary public within the state:

(1) every member of the legislature, while still a resident in the district from which elected; but no fee or compensation may be received for exercising these powers. The form of the official signature in these cases is: "A.B., Representative (or Senator), _____ District, Minnesota, ex officio notary public. My term expires January 1, _____";

(2) the clerks or recorders of towns, and cities. The form of the official signature in these cases is: "A.B. (official title), ... County, Minnesota, ex officio notary public. My term expires .... (or where applicable) my term is indeterminate.";

(3) court commissioners, county recorders, and county auditors, and their several deputies, and county commissioners, all within their respective counties. The form of the official signature in these cases: "A.B. (official title), ... County, Minnesota, ex officio notary public. My term expires .... (or where applicable) my term is indeterminate."; and

(4) peace officers licensed under section 626.845 for the purpose of administering oaths upon information submitted to establish probable cause to any judge or judicial officer under the Rules of Criminal Procedure. The form of the official signature in these cases is "A.B., Peace Officer License Number _____, _____ County, Minnesota. My License expires June 30, _____".

(b) An officer using the powers of a notary public within the state pursuant to clauses (1) to (3) shall obtain an official stamp as specified under section 359.03, subdivisions 1, 3, and 4, with which to authenticate official acts.

(c) The county auditor and county recorder, and their deputies, and the clerk or recorder of a town or city with ex officio powers under this section may authenticate official acts related to the statutory duties of their respective offices without using the official stamp for 90 days after initially assuming the office, or until the officer acquires an official stamp, whichever is earlier.

EFFECTIVE DATE; APPLICABILITY. This section is effective August 1, 2010, except that an officer with ex officio powers subject to paragraph (c) may authenticate official acts related to the officer's statutory duties without using the official stamp for up to 90 days after the effective date of this section, or until the officer acquires an official stamp, whichever is earlier.

History: (6973) RL s 2687; 1973 c 123 art 5 s 7; 1976 c 181 s 2; 1983 c 359 s 45; 1985 c 268 s 1; 1995 c 37 s 1; 2010 c 380 s 4

358.16-358.21 Obsolete

358.22 Repealed, 1973 c 116 s 10

358.23 Repealed, 1973 c 116 s 10

358.24 Repealed, 1973 c 116 s 10

358.25 Power given for taking acknowledgments for protesting bills of exchange.

Any person authorized to take acknowledgments or administer oaths, who is at the same time an officer, director or stockholder of a corporation, is hereby authorized to take acknowledgments of instruments wherein such corporation is interested, and to administer oaths to any officer, director, or stockholder of such corporation as such, and to protest for nonacceptance or nonpayment bills of exchange, drafts, checks, notes and other negotiable or nonnegotiable instruments which may be owned or held for collection by such corporation, as fully and effectually as if the person were not an officer, director, or stockholder of such corporation.

History: (6980) 1907 c 406 s 1; 1915 c 20 s 1; 1986 c 444

358.26 Repealed, 1973 c 116 s 10

358.27 Repealed, 1973 c 116 s 10

358.271 Obsolete

358.28-358.31 Obsolete

358.32 Repealed, 1985 c 268 s 12

358.33 Repealed, 1985 c 268 s 12

358.34 Repealed, 1985 c 268 s 12

358.35 Repealed, 1985 c 268 s 12

358.36 Repealed, 1985 c 268 s 12

358.37 Repealed, 1985 c 268 s 12

358.38 Repealed, 1985 c 268 s 12

358.39 Repealed, 1985 c 268 s 12

358.40 Repealed, 1985 c 268 s 12

358.41 Definitions.
As used in sections 358.41 to 358.49:

(1) "Notarial act" means any act that a notary public of this state is authorized to perform, and includes taking an acknowledgment, administering an oath or affirmation, taking a verification upon oath or affirmation, witnessing or attesting a signature, certifying or attesting a copy, and noting a protest of a negotiable instrument. A notary public may perform a notarial act by electronic means.

(2) "Acknowledgment" means a declaration by a person that the person has executed an instrument or electronic record for the purposes stated therein and, if the instrument or electronic record is executed in a representative capacity, that the person signed the instrument with proper authority and executed it as the act of the person or entity represented and identified therein.

(3) "Verification upon oath or affirmation" means a declaration that a statement is true made by a person upon oath or affirmation.

(4) "In a representative capacity" means:

(i) for and on behalf of a corporation, partnership, limited liability company, trust, or other entity, as an authorized officer, agent, partner, trustee, or other representative;

(ii) as a public officer, personal representative, guardian, or other representative, in the capacity recited in the instrument;

(iii) as an attorney in fact for a principal; or

(iv) in any other capacity as an authorized representative of another.

(5) "Notarial officer" means a notary public or other officer authorized to perform notarial acts.

(6) "Electronic signature" means an electronic sound, symbol, or process attached to or logically associated with a record and executed or adopted by a person with the intent to sign the record.

(7) "Electronic record" means a record created, generated, sent, communicated, received, or stored by electronic means.

History: 1985 c 268 s 2; 2006 c 260 s 1; 2007 c 148 s 63

358.42 Notarial acts.

(a) In taking an acknowledgment, the notarial officer must determine, either from personal knowledge or from satisfactory evidence, that the person appearing before the officer and making the acknowledgment is the person whose true signature is on the instrument or electronic record.

(b) In taking a verification upon oath or affirmation, the notarial officer must determine, either from personal knowledge or from satisfactory evidence, that the person appearing before the officer and making the verification is the person whose true signature is made in the presence of the officer on the statement verified.

(c) In witnessing or attesting a signature the notarial officer must determine, either from personal knowledge or from satisfactory evidence, that the signature is that of the person appearing before the officer and named therein. When witnessing or attesting a signature, the officer must be present when the signature is made.

(d) In certifying or attesting a copy of a document, electronic record, or other item, the notarial officer must determine that the proffered copy is a full, true, and accurate transcription or reproduction of that which was copied.

(e) In making or noting a protest of a negotiable instrument or electronic record the notarial officer must determine the matters set forth in section 336.3-505.

(f) A notarial officer has satisfactory evidence that a person is the person whose true signature is on a document or electronic record if that person:

(i) is personally known to the notarial officer,

(ii) is identified upon the oath or affirmation of a credible witness personally known to the notarial officer, or

(iii) is identified on the basis of identification documents.

History: 1985 c 268 s 3; 1992 c 565 s 113; 2006 c 260 s 2; 2007 c 148 s 64

358.43 Notarial acts in this state.

(a) A notarial act may be performed within this state by the following persons:

(1) a notary public of this state,

(2) a judge, court administrator, or deputy court administrator of any court of this state,

(3) a person authorized by the law of this state to administer oaths, or

(4) any other person authorized to perform the specific act by the law of this state.

(b) Notarial acts performed within this state under federal authority as provided in section 358.45 have the same effect as if performed by a notarial officer of this state.

(c) The signature and title of a person performing a notarial act are prima facie evidence that the signature is genuine and that the person holds the designated title.
History: 1985 c 268 s 4; 1Sp1986 c 3 art 1 s 82; 1992 c 464 art 1 s 56

358.44 Notarial acts in other jurisdictions of the United States.

(a) A notarial act has the same effect under the law of this state as if performed by a notarial officer of this state, if performed in another state, commonwealth, territory, district, or possession of the United States by any of the following persons:

(1) a notary public of that jurisdiction;

(2) a judge, clerk, or deputy clerk of a court of that jurisdiction; or

(3) any other person authorized by the law of that jurisdiction to perform notarial acts.

(b) Notarial acts performed in other jurisdictions of the United States under federal authority as provided in section 358.45 have the same effect as if performed by a notarial officer of this state.

(c) The signature and title of a person performing a notarial act are prima facie evidence that the signature is genuine and that the person holds the designated title.

(d) The signature and indicated title of an officer listed in subsection (a)(1) or (a)(2) conclusively establish the authority of a holder of that title to perform a notarial act.

History: 1985 c 268 s 5; 1Sp1986 c 3 art 1 s 47

358.45 Notarial acts under federal authority.

(a) A notarial act has the same effect under the law of this state as if performed by a notarial officer of this state if performed anywhere by any of the following persons under authority granted by the law of the United States:

(1) a judge, clerk, or deputy clerk of a court;

(2) a commissioned officer on active duty in the military service of the United States;

(3) an officer of the foreign service or consular officer of the United States; or

(4) any other person authorized by federal law to perform notarial acts.

(b) The signature and title of a person performing a notarial act are prima facie evidence that the signature is genuine and that the person holds the designated title.

(c) The signature and indicated title of an officer listed in subsection (a)(1), (a)(2), or (a)(3) conclusively establish the authority of a holder of that title to perform a notarial act.

History: 1985 c 268 s 6

358.46 Foreign notarial acts.

(a) A notarial act has the same effect under the law of this state as if performed by a notarial officer of this state if performed within the jurisdiction of and under authority of a foreign nation or its constituent units or a multinational or international organization by any of the following persons:

(1) a notary public or notary;

(2) a judge, clerk, or deputy clerk of a court of record; or

(3) any other person authorized by the law of that jurisdiction to perform notarial acts.

(b) An "Apostille" in the form prescribed by the Hague Convention of October 5, 1961, conclusively establishes that the signature of the notarial officer is genuine and that the officer holds the indicated office.

(c) A certificate by a foreign service or consular officer of the United States stationed in the nation under the jurisdiction of which the notarial act was performed, or a certificate by a foreign service or consular officer of that nation stationed in the United States, conclusively establishes any matter relating to the authenticity or validity of the notarial act set forth in the certificate.

(d) An official stamp or seal of the person performing the notarial act is prima facie evidence that the signature is genuine and that the person holds the indicated title.

(e) An official stamp or seal of an officer listed in subsection (a)(l) or (a)(2) is prima facie evidence that a person with the indicated title has authority to perform notarial acts.

(f) If the title of office and indication of authority to perform notarial acts appears either in a digest of foreign law or in a list customarily used as a source for that information, the authority of an officer with that title to perform notarial acts is conclusively established.

History: 1985 c 268 s 7

358.47 Certificate of notarial acts.

(a) A notarial act must be evidenced by a certificate physically or electronically signed and dated by a notarial officer in a manner that attributes such signature to the notary public identified on the commission. The notary's name as it appears on the official notarial stamp and on any jurat or certificate of acknowledgment and in the notary's commission must be identical. The certificate must include identification of the jurisdiction in which the notarial act is performed and the title of the office of the notarial officer and may must include the official notarial stamp or seal of office, or the notary's electronic seal pursuant to section 359.03. If the officer is a notary public, the certificate must also indicate the date of expiration, if any, of the commission of office, but omission of that information may subsequently be corrected. If the officer is a commissioned officer on active duty in the military service of the United States, it must also include the officer's rank.

(b) A certificate of a notarial act is sufficient if it is in English and meets the requirements of subsection (a) and it: (1) is in the short form set forth in section 358.48;

(2) is in a form otherwise prescribed by the law of this state;

(3) is in a form prescribed by the laws or regulations applicable in the place in which the notarial act was performed; or

(4) sets forth the actions of the notarial officer and those are sufficient to meet the requirements of the designated notarial act.

(c) By executing a certificate of a notarial act, the notarial officer certifies that the officer has made the determinations required by section 358.42.

History: 1985 c 268 s 8; 2006 c 260 s 3 ; 2010 c 380 s 5

358.48 Short forms.

The following short form certificates of notarial acts are sufficient for the purposes indicated, it completed with the information required by section 358.47, subsection (a):

(1) For an acknowledgment in an individual capacity:

State of _____
County of _____

This instrument was acknowledged before me on _____ (date) by _____ (name[s] of person[s]).

_____
(Signature of notarial officer)

Title (and Rank) _____   (Stamp)

My commission expires: _____

(2) For an acknowledgment in a representative capacity:

State of _____
County of _____

This instrument was acknowledged before me on _____ (date) by _____ (name[s] of person[s]) as _____ (type of authority, e.g., officer, trustee, etc.) of _____ (name of party on behalf of whom the instrument was executed).

_____
(Signature of notarial officer)

Title (and Rank) _____   (Stamp)

My commission expires: _____

(3) For a verification upon oath or affirmation:

State of _____
County of _____

Signed and sworn to (or affirmed) before me on _____ (date) by _____ (name[s] of person[s] making statement).

_____
(Signature of notarial officer)

Title (and Rank) _____   (Stamp)

My commission expires: _____

(4) For witnessing or attesting a signature:

State of _____
County of _____

Signed or attested before me on _____ (date) by
_____ (name[s]) of person[s]).

_____
(Signature of notarial officer)

Title (and Rank) _____   (Stamp)

My commission expires: _____

(5) For attestation of a copy of a document:

State of _____
County of _____

I certify that this is a true and correct copy of a document in the possession of
_____.

Dated: _____

_____
(Signature of notarial officer)

Title (and Rank) _____   (Stamp)

My commission expires: _____

History: 1985 c 268 s 9

358.49 Short title.
Sections 358.41 to 358.49 may be cited as the uniform law on notarial acts.
History: 1985 c 268 s 10

358.50 Effect of acknowledgment.
An acknowledgment made in a representative capacity for and on behalf of a corporation, partnership, limited liability company, trust, or other entity and certified substantially in the form prescribed in this chapter is prima facie evidence that the instrument or electronic record was executed and delivered with proper authority.
History: 1987 c 26 s 1; 2006 c 260 s 4; 2007 c 148 s 65

MINNESOTA NOTARY LAW PRIMER

CHAPTER 359. NOTARIES PUBLIC

359.01 Commission.

Subdivision 1. Resident notaries. The governor may appoint and commission as notaries public, by and with the advice and consent of the senate, as many citizens of this state or resident aliens, over the age of 18 years, as the governor considers necessary. The governor will appoint and commission notaries public and the secretary of state shall receive applications for appointments and commissions, shall keep a register of those persons appointed and commissioned as notaries public by the governor with the advice and consent of the senate, shall update that register when informed of a change in name and address by a notary public, shall process applications by a notary public for reappointment, shall receive fees for the performance of these functions to be deposited into the general fund, and shall perform those clerical and administrative duties associated with these functions. The governor may also receive such applications directly.

Subd. 2. Nonresident notaries. (a) The governor, by and with the consent of the senate, may appoint as notary public a person who is not a resident of this state if:

(1) the person is a resident of Wisconsin, Iowa, North Dakota, or South Dakota;

(2) the person designates the secretary of state as agent for the service of process for all purposes relating to notarial acts and for receipt of all correspondence relating to notarial acts; and

(3) the person designates the Minnesota county in which the person's notary commission will be recorded pursuant to section 359.061.

(b) The secretary of state shall receive applications for nonresident notary appointments and commissions, shall keep a register of those persons appointed and commissioned as notaries public by the governor with the advice and consent of the senate, shall update that register when informed of a change in name and address by a notary public, shall process applications by a notary public for reappointment, shall receive fees for the performance of these functions to be deposited into the general fund, and shall perform those clerical and administrative duties associated with these functions. The governor may also receive such applications directly.

Subd. 3. Fees.(a) When making application for a commission the applicant must submit, along with the information required by the secretary of state, a nonrefundable fee of $120, which shall be forwarded by the secretary of state to the commissioner of management and budget to be deposited in the state treasury and credited to the general fund.

(b) Except as otherwise provided in paragraph (a), all fees shall be retained by the secretary of state and are nonreturnable, except for an overpayment of a fee.

Subd. 4. Application. The secretary of state shall prepare the application form for a commission. The form may request personal information about the applicant, including, but not limited to, relevant civil litigation, occupational license history, and criminal background, if any. For the purposes of this section, "criminal background" includes, but is not limited to, criminal charges, arrests, indictments, pleas, and convictions.

Subd. 5. Registration to perform electronic notarizations. Before performing electronic notarial acts, a notary public shall register the capability to notarize electronically with the secretary of state. Before performing electronic notarial acts after recommissioning, a notary public shall reregister with the secretary of state.

History: (6937) RL s 2656; 1955 c 820 s 44; 1969 c 1148 s 59; 1973 c 725 s 67; 1984 c 504 s 1; 1984 c 609 s 23: 1984 c 654 art 2 s 129; 1Sp1986 c 3 art 1 s 82; 1992 c 513 art 3 s 72; 1993 c 354 s 2; 1993 c 369 s 127; 1996 c 439 art 1 s 22, 23; 2004 c 251 art 1 s 19; 2005 c 156 a 2 s 37; 2006 c 260 s 5; 2009 c 101 art 2 s 88; 2010 c 380 s 7, 8

359.02 Term.

A notary commissioned under section 359.01 holds office until January 31 of the fifth year following the year the commission was issued, unless sooner removed by the governor or the district court, or by action of the commissioner of commerce.

Six months before the expiration of the commission, a notary may renew the notary's commission for a new term to commence and to be designated in the new commission as beginning upon the day immediately following the date of the expiration. A notary whose commission expires may apply for reappointment after the expiration date. The reappointment or renewal takes effect and is valid although the appointing governor may not be in the Office of Governor on the effective day.

EFFECTIVE DATE. The provisions of this section relating to the time during which a notary's commission may be renewed are effective July 31, 2011. The remainder of this section is effective August 1, 2010.

(a) All notary commissions issued before January 31, 1995, will expire on January 31, 1995.

(b) All notary commissions issued after January 31, 1995, will expire at the end of the licensing period, which will end every fifth year following January 31, 1995.

(c) All notary commissions issued during a licensing period expire at the end of that period as set forth in this section.

History: (6938) RL s 2657; 1953 c 63 s 1; 1984 c 504 s 2; 1986 c 444; 1989 c 6 s 1; 1989 c 189 s 1; 1993 c 354 s 3; 1993 c 369 s 128; 1994 c 465 art 3 s 72; 1996 c 439 art 1 s 24;2010 c 380 s 9

359.03 Seal; register.

Subdivision 1. Requirement. Every notary, including an ex officio notary under section 358.15, shall obtain an official notarial stamp as specified in subdivision 3, with which to authenticate official acts. The official notarial stamp, and the notary's official journal, are the personal property of the notary and are exempt from execution.

Subd. 2. Validation and legalization of certain instruments. (a) All instruments heretofore duly made and executed which have been acknowledged before a notary public as provided by law, but the seal or stamp used thereon has engraved on it "notary public," are hereby validated and legalized, and in case such instruments are recorded, the recording is hereby validated and legalized, and all such instruments are validated to the same extent as though properly sealed at the time of their acknowledgment. This subdivision shall not affect any action now pending in any of the courts of this state.

(b) The official notarial stamp required by this section, whether applied to the record physically or electronically, is deemed to be a "seal" for purposes of the admission of a document in court.

Subd. 3. Specifications. The official notarial stamp consists of the seal of the state of Minnesota, the name of the notary as it appears on the commission or the name of the ex officio notary, the words "Notary Public," or "Notarial Officer" in the case of an ex officio notary, and the words "My commission expires................ (or where applicable) My term is indeterminate," with the expiration date shown on it and must be able to be reproduced in any legibly reproducible manner. The official notarial stamp shall be a rectangular form of not more than three-fourths of an inch vertically by 2-1/2 inches horizontally, with a serrated or milled edge border, and shall contain the information required by this subdivision.

Subd. 4. Notarial stamp may be affixed electronically. The information required by this section may be affixed electronically and shall be logically and securely affixed or associated with the electronic record being notarized.

History: (6939) RL s 2658; 1947 c 42 s 1; 1947 c 372 s 1; 1971 c 251 s 1; 1986 c 441; 1Sp1986 c 3 art 1 s 82; 1993 c 354 s 4, 5; 2006 c 260 s 6, 7; 2010 c 380 s 10-13

359.04 Powers.

Every notary public so appointed, commissioned, and qualified shall have power throughout this state to administer all oaths required or authorized to be administered in this state; to take and certify all depositions to be used in any of the courts of this state; to take and certify all acknowledgments of deeds, mortgages, liens, powers of attorney, and other instruments in writing or electronic records; and to receive, make out, and record notarial protests.

History: (6940) RL s 2659; 1947 c 372 s 2; 1993 c 354 s 6; 2006 c 260 art 7 s 8

359.05 Repealed, 2010 c 380 s 18

359.06 Repealed, 1976 c 2 s 128

359.061 Record of Commission.

Subdivision 1. Resident notaries. The commission of every notary commissioned under section 359.01, together with: (1) a signature that matches the first, middle, and last name as listed on the notary's commission and shown on the notarial stamp, and (2) a sample signature in the style in which the notary will actually execute notarial acts, shall be recorded in the office of the local registrar of the notary's county of residence or in the county department to which duties relating to notaries public have been assigned under section 485.27, in a record kept for that purpose.

Subd. 2. **Nonresident notaries.** The commission of a nonresident notary must be recorded in the Minnesota county the notary designates pursuant to section 359.01, subdivision 2, clause (3), in the county department to which duties relating to notaries public have been assigned under section 485.27.

Subd. 3. **Certificate of court administrator.** The court administrator, when requested, shall certify to official acts in the manner and for the fees prescribed by statute or court rule.

Subd. 4. **County notary certificate.** The county department, to which duties relating to notaries public have been assigned under section 485.27, shall certify to official acts under this section for the fee of $5 and in the form of:

State of Minnesota .... County
"I the undersigned ...., in and for said county and state, do hereby certify that ...., whose name is subscribed to on the attached document held the office of notary public in said county and state at the date of said subscription and was authorized under the laws of this state to take acknowledgments, to administer oaths, take depositions, acknowledgments of deeds, and other written instruments, and exercise all such powers and duties authorized by the laws of Minnesota as notary public. I further certify that I have compared the subscribed signature to the signature on file in this office and believe them to be the same.
Signed this date .... in the county of ...., state of Minnesota."
Signature ....
Title ....

History: 1976 c 239 s 109; 1983 c 359 s 46; 1986 c 444; 1Sp1986 c 3 art 1 s 82; 1996 c 439 art 1 s 25; 1997 c 222 s 55; 2010 c 380 s 14

359.062 Notice; languages other than English.

(a) A notary public who is not an attorney who advertises the services of a notary public in a language other than English, whether by radio, television, signs, pamphlets, newspapers, or other written communication, with the exception of a single desk plaque, shall post or otherwise include with the advertisement a notice in English and the language in which the advertisement appears. This notice must be of a conspicuous size, if in writing, and must state: "I AM NOT AN ATTORNEY LICENSED TO PRACTICE LAW IN MINNESOTA, AND MAY NOT GIVE LEGAL ADVICE OR ACCEPT FEES FOR LEGAL ADVICE." If the advertisement is by radio or television, the statement may be modified but must include substantially the same message.

(b) A notary public who violates this section is guilty of a misdemeanor.

History: 1996 c 401 s 2

359.07 Notary in detached county.

Subdivision 1. **Powers.** In any county which has heretofore been detached from another county of this state, and which has been newly created and organized, any notary public residing in such newly created and organized county, who was a resident of the county from which the new county was detached and created, shall have the same powers during the unexpired term of appointment as such notary public was authorized by law to exercise under the commission issued to the notary as a resident of the county from which the new county was detached and created and within which the original appointment as notary public was made; and all acts heretofore done by any such notary public, while residing in the newly created and organized county, otherwise in conformity of law, are hereby declared to be legal and valid and to the same effect as if the notary public had been originally commissioned as a resident of the newly created and organized county.

Subd. 2. Record of commission. Such notary public so residing in the newly created and organized county shall have the commission as such notary public recorded by the court administrator of the district court of the newly created and organized county of residence, or of the county to which the newly created county is attached for judicial purposes, as provided in section 359.061, and when so recorded shall be entitled to the same certificate of and from the court administrator of the district court as provided in section 359.061.

Subd. 3. Seal. Such notary shall, immediately upon the adoption of this section, get an official seal, as provided in and in conformity with section 359.03.

History: (6943, 6944, 6945) 1907 c 323 s 1-3; 1980 c 509 s 142; 1986 c 444; LSp1986 c 3 art 1 s 82

359.071 Change of name or address.

A notary shall notify the secretary of state of any name or address change within 30 days of the change.

History: 1984 c 504 s 3; 1986 c 444; 1989 c 189 s 2; 1993 c 354 s 8; 1997 c 222 s 56A; 2004 c 251 s 20

359.08 Misconduct.

Any notary who shall exercise the duties of office after the expiration of a term, or when otherwise disqualified, shall be guilty of a misdemeanor.

History: (6946) RL s 2661; 1963 c 753 art 2 s 5; 1986 c 444

359.085 Standards of conduct for notarial acts.

Subdivision 1. Acknowledgments. In taking an acknowledgment, the notarial officer must determine, either from personal knowledge or from satisfactory evidence, that the person appearing before the officer and making the acknowledgment is the person whose true signature is on the instrument or electronic record.

Subd. 2. Verifications. In taking a verification upon oath or affirmation, the notarial officer must determine, either from personal knowledge or from satisfactory evidence, that the person appearing before the officer and making the verification is the person whose true signature is made in the presence of the officer on the statement verified.

Subd. 3. Witnessing or attesting signatures. In witnessing or attesting a signature, the notarial officer must determine, either from personal knowledge or from satisfactory evidence, that the signature is that of the person appearing before the officer and named in the document or electronic record. When witnessing or attesting a signature, the officer must be present when the signature is made.

Subd. 4. Certifying or attesting documents. In certifying or attesting a copy of a document, electronic record, or other item, the notarial officer must determine that the proffered copy is a full, true, and accurate transcription or reproduction of that which was copied.

Subd. 5. Making or noting protests of negotiable instruments. In making or noting a protest of a negotiable instrument or electronic record, the notarial officer must determine the matters set forth in section 336.3-505.

Subd. 6. Satisfactory evidence. A notarial officer has satisfactory evidence that a person is the person whose true signature is on a document or electronic record if that person (i) is personally known to the notarial officer, (ii) is identified upon the oath or affirmation of a credible witness personally known to the notarial officer, or (iii) is identified on the basis of identification documents.

Subd. 7. Prohibited acts. A notarial officer may not acknowledge, witness or attest to the officer's own signature, or take a verification of the officer's own oath or affirmation.

Subd. 8. Repealed, 2007 c 148 art 2 s 84

History: 2000 c 483 s 53; 2006 c 260 s 10; 2007 c 148 s 66, 67

359.09 Repealed, 1965 c 811 art 10 s 336.10-102

359.091 Accommodation of physical limitations.

(a) A notary public may certify as to the subscription or signature of an individual when it appears that the individual has a physical limitation that restricts the individual's ability to sign by writing or making a mark, pursuant to the following:

(1) the name of an individual may be signed, or attached electronically in the case of an electronic record, by another individual other than the notary public at the direction and in the presence of the individual whose name is to be signed and in the presence of the notary public. The signature may be made by a rubber stamp facsimile of the person's actual signature, mark, or a signature of the person's name or mark made by another and adopted for all purposes of signature by the person with a physical limitation; and

(2) the words "Signature written by" or "Signature attached by" in the case of an electronic record, "(name of individual directed to sign or directed to attach) at the direction and in the presence of (name as signed) on whose behalf the signature was written" or "attached electronically" in the case of an electronic record, or words of substantially similar effect must appear under or near the signature.

(b) A notary public may use signals or electronic or mechanical means to take an acknowledgment from, administer an oath or affirmation to, or otherwise communicate with any individual in the presence of such notary public when it appears that the individual is unable to communicate verbally or in writing.

359.10 Repealed, 1965 c 811 art 10 s 336.10-102

359.11 Taking depositions.
In taking depositions, the notary shall have the power to compel the attendance of and to punish witnesses for refusing to testify as provided by statute or court rule. All sheriffs and constables shall serve and return all process issued by any notary in taking depositions.
History: (6949) RL s 2664; 1983 c 359 s 47; 2005 c 10 art 2 s 4

359.12 Administrative actions and penalties.
Every notary who shall charge or receive a fee or reward for any act or service done or rendered as a notary greater than the amount allowed by law, or who dishonestly or unfaithfully discharges duties as notary, or who has pleaded guilty, with or without explicitly admitting guilt, plead[ed] nolo contendere, or been convicted of a felony, gross misdemeanor, or misdemeanor involving moral turpitude, is subject to the penalties imposed pursuant to section 45.027. A notary may be removed from office only by the governor, the district court, or the commissioner of commerce. The commissioner of commerce has all the powers provided by section 45.027 and shall proceed in the manner provided by that section in actions against notaries.

Notwithstanding section 359.03, subdivision 1, upon removal from office by the commissioner of commerce, a notary public shall deliver the notary's official notarial stamp to the commissioner of commerce.
***
History: (6950) RL s 2665; 1986 c 444; 1Sp1986 c 3 art 1 s 82; 1993 c 354 s 9; 2010 c 380 s 16

CHAPTER 45. DEPARTMENT OF COMMERCE: GENERAL POWERS

45.027 Investigations and subpoenas.
Subdivision 1. General powers. In connection with the duties and responsibilities entrusted to the commissioner, and Laws 1993, chapter 361, section 2, the commissioner of commerce may:

(1) make public or private investigations within or without this state as the commissioner considers necessary to determine whether any person has violated or is about to violate any law, rule, or order related to the duties and responsibilities entrusted to the commissioner;

(2) require or permit any person to file a statement in writing, under oath or otherwise as the commissioner determines, as to all the facts and circumstances concerning the matter being investigated;

(3) hold hearings, upon reasonable notice, in respect to any matter arising out of the duties and responsibilities entrusted to the commissioner;

(4) conduct investigations and hold hearings for the purpose of compiling information related to the duties and responsibilities entrusted to the commissioner;

(5) examine the books, accounts, records, and files of every licensee, and of every person who is engaged in any activity regulated; the commissioner or a designated representative shall have free access during normal business hours to the offices and places of business of the person, and to all books, accounts, papers, records, files, safes, and vaults maintained in the place of business;

(6) publish information which is contained in any order issued by the commissioner;

(7) require any person subject to duties and responsibilities entrusted to the commissioner, to report all sales or transactions that are regulated. The reports must be made within ten days after the commissioner has ordered the report. The report is accessible only to the respondent and other governmental agencies unless otherwise ordered by a court of competent jurisdiction; and

(8) assess a natural person or entity subject to the jurisdiction of the commissioner the necessary expenses of the investigation performed by the department when an investigation is made by order of the commissioner. The cost of the investigation shall be determined by the commissioner and is based on the salary cost of investigators or assistants and at an average rate per day or fraction thereof so as to provide for the total cost of the investigation. All money collected must be deposited into the general fund. A natural person licensed under chapter 60K or 82 shall not be charged costs of an investigation if the investigation results in no finding of a violation.

Subd. 1a. Response to department requests. An applicant, registrant, certificate holder, licensee, or other person subject to the jurisdiction of the commissioner shall comply with requests for information, documents, or other requests from the department within the time specified in the request, or, if no time is specified, within 30 days of the mailing of the request by the department. Applicants, registrants, certificate holders, licensees, or other persons subject to the jurisdiction of the commissioner shall appear before the commissioner or the commissioner's representative when requested to do so and shall bring all documents or materials that the commissioner or the commissioner's representative has requested.

Subd. 2. Power to compel production of evidence. For the purpose of any investigation, hearing, proceeding, or inquiry related to the duties and responsibilities entrusted to the commissioner, the commissioner or a designated representative may administer oaths and affirmations, subpoena witnesses, compel their attendance, take evidence, and require the production of books, papers, correspondence, memoranda, agreements, or other documents or records that the commissioner considers relevant or material to the inquiry.

Subd. 3. Court orders. In case of a refusal to appear or a refusal to obey a subpoena issued to any person, the district court, upon application by the commissioner, may issue to any person an order directing that person to appear before the commissioner, or the officer designated by the commissioner, there to produce documentary evidence if so ordered or to give evidence relating to the matter under investigation or in question. Failure to obey the order of the court may be punished by the court as a contempt of court.

Subd. 4. Scope of privilege. No person is excused from attending and testifying or from producing any document or record before the commissioner, or from obedience to the subpoena of the commissioner or any officer designated by the commissioner or in a proceeding instituted by the commissioner, on the ground that the testimony or evidence required may tend to incriminate that person or subject that person to a penalty of forfeiture. No person may be prosecuted or subjected to a penalty or forfeiture for or on account of a transaction, matter, or thing concerning which the person is compelled, after claiming the privilege against self-incrimination, to testify or produce evidence, documentary or otherwise, except that the individual is not exempt from prosecution and punishment for perjury or contempt committed in testifying.

Subd. 5. Legal actions; injunctions. Whenever it appears to the commissioner that any person has engaged or is about to engage in any act or practice constituting a violation of any law, rule, or order related to the duties and responsibilities entrusted to the commissioner, the commissioner may bring an action in the name of the state in Ramsey County District Court or the district court of an appropriate county to enjoin the acts or practices and to enforce compliance, or the commissioner may refer the matter to the attorney general or the county attorney of the appropriate county. A permanent injunction or other appropriate relief must be granted based solely upon a showing that the person has engaged or is about to engage in an act or practice constituting a violation of a law, rule, cease and desist order, or other order related to the duties and responsibilities entrusted to the commissioner. The terms of this subdivision govern an action brought under this subdivision, including an action against a person who, for whatever reason, claims that the subject law, rule, cease and desist order or other order does not apply to the person.

Subd. 5a. Cease and desist orders.

(a) Whenever it appears to the commissioner that a person has engaged or is about to engage in an act or practice constituting a violation of a law, rule, or order related to the duties and responsibilities entrusted to the commissioner, the commissioner may issue and cause to be served upon the person an order requiring the person to cease and desist from violations.

(b) The cease and desist order must be calculated to give reasonable notice of the rights of the person to request a hearing and must state the reasons for the entry of the order. A hearing must be held not later than ten days after the request for the hearing is received by the commissioner. After the completion of the hearing, the administrative law judge shall issue a report within ten days. Within 15 days after receiving the administrative law judge's report, the commissioner shall issue a further order vacating or making permanent the cease and desist order. The time periods provided in this provision may be waived by agreement of the person requesting the hearing and the Department of Commerce and the person against whom the cease and desist order is issued. If the person to whom a cease and desist order is issued fails to appear at the hearing after being duly notified, the person is in default, and the proceeding may be determined against that person upon consideration of the cease and desist order, the allegations of which may be considered to be true. Unless otherwise provided, all hearings must be conducted according to chapter 14. The commissioner may adopt rules of procedure concerning all proceedings conducted under this subdivision.

(c) If no hearing is requested within 30 days of service of the order, the cease and desist order will become permanent.

(d) A cease and desist order issued under this subdivision remains in effect until it is modified or vacated by the commissioner. The administrative proceeding provided by this subdivision, and subsequent appellate judicial review of that administrative proceeding, constitutes the exclusive remedy for determining whether the commissioner properly issued the cease and desist order and whether the cease and desist order should be vacated or made permanent.

Subd. 5b. Enforcement of violations of cease and desist orders.

(a) Whenever the commissioner under subdivision 5 seeks to enforce compliance with a cease and desist order that has been made permanent, the allegations in the cease and desist order are considered conclusively established for purposes of a proceeding under subdivision 5 for permanent or temporary relief to enforce the cease and desist order. Whenever the commissioner under subdivision 5 seeks to enforce compliance with a cease and desist order when a hearing or hearing request on the cease and desist order is pending, or the time has not yet expired to request a hearing on whether a cease and desist order should be vacated or made permanent, the allegations in the cease and desist order are considered conclusively established for purposes of a proceeding under subdivision 5 for temporary relief to enforce the cease and desist order.

(b) Notwithstanding this subdivision or subdivision 5 or 5a to the contrary, the person against whom the cease and desist order is issued and who has requested a hearing under subdivision 5a may within 15 days after service of cease and desist order bring an action in Ramsey County District Court for issuance of an injunction to suspend enforcement of the cease and desist order pending a final decision of the commissioner under subdivision 5a to vacate or make permanent the cease and desist order. The court shall determine whether to issue such an injunction based on traditional principles of temporary relief.

Subd. 6. Violations and penalties. The commissioner may impose a civil penalty not to exceed $10,000 per violation upon a person who violates any law, rule, or order related to the duties and responsibilities entrusted to the commissioner unless a different penalty is specified. If a civil penalty is imposed on a health carrier as defined in section 62A.011, the commissioner must divide 50 percent of the amount among any policy holders or certificate holders affected by the violation, unless the commissioner certifies in writing that the division and distribution to enrollees would be too administratively complex or that the number of enrollees affected by the penalty would result in a distribution of less than $50 per enrollee.

Subd. 7. Actions against licensees.

(a) In addition to any other actions authorized by this section, the commissioner may, by order, deny, suspend, or revoke the authority or license of a person subject to the duties and responsibilities entrusted to the commissioner, as described under section 45.011, subdivision 4, or censure that person if the commissioner finds that:

(1) the order is in the public interest; and

(2) the person has violated any law, rule, or order related to the duties and responsibilities entrusted to the commissioner; or

(3) the person has provided false, misleading, or incomplete information to the commissioner or has refused to allow a reasonable inspection of records or premises; or

(4) the person has engaged in an act or practice, whether or not the act or practice directly involves the business for which the person is licensed or authorized, which demonstrates that the applicant or licensee is untrustworthy, financially irresponsible, or otherwise incompetent or unqualified to act under the authority or license granted by the commissioner.

(b) The commissioner shall issue an order requiring a licensee or applicant for a license to show cause why the license should not be revoked or suspended, or the licensee censured, or the application denied. The order must be calculated to give reasonable notice of the time and place for a hearing on the action, and must state the reasons for the entry of the order. The commissioner may, by order, summarily suspend a license pending final determination of an order to show cause. If a license is suspended pending final determination of an order to show cause, a hearing on the merits must be held within 30 days of the issuance of the order of suspension. All hearings must be conducted according to chapter 14. After the hearing, the commissioner shall enter an order disposing of the matter as the facts require. If the licensee or applicant fails to appear at a hearing after having been duly notified of it, the person is considered in default, and the proceeding may be determined against the licensee or applicant upon consideration of the order to show cause, the allegations of which may be considered true. The summary suspension or summary revocation procedures does not apply to action by the commissioner against the certificate of authority of an insurer authorized to do business in Minnesota.

Except for information classified as confidential under sections 60A.03, subdivision 9; 60A.031; 60A.93; and 60D.22, the commissioner may make any data otherwise classified as private or confidential pursuant to this section accessible to an appropriate person or agency if the commissioner determines that the access will aid the law enforcement process, promote public health or safety, or dispel widespread rumor or unrest. If the commissioner determines that private or confidential information should be disclosed, the commissioner shall notify the attorney general as to the information to be disclosed, the purpose of the disclosure, and the need for the disclosure. The attorney general shall review the commissioner's determination. If the attorney general believes that the commissioner's determination does not satisfy the purpose and intent of this provision, the attorney general shall advise the commissioner in writing that the information may not be disclosed. If the attorney general believes the commissioner's determination satisfies the purpose and intent of this provision, the attorney general shall advise the commissioner in writing, accordingly.

After disclosing information pursuant to this provision, the commissioner shall advise the chairs of the senate and house of representatives judiciary committees of the disclosure and the basis for it.

Subd. 7a. Authorized disclosures of information and data.

(a) The commissioner may release and disclose any active or inactive investigative information and data to any national securities exchange or national securities association registered under the Securities Exchange Act of 1934 when necessary for the requesting agency in initiating, furthering, or completing an investigation.

(b) The commissioner may release any active or inactive investigative data relating to the conduct of the business of insurance to the Office of the Comptroller of the Currency or the Office of Thrift Supervision in order to facilitate the initiation, furtherance, or completion of the investigation.

Subd. 8. Stop order. In addition to any other actions authorized by this section, the commissioner may issue a stop order denying effectiveness to or suspending or revoking any registration.

Subd. 9. Powers additional. The powers contained in subdivisions 1 to 8 are in addition to all other powers of the commissioner.

Subd. 10. Rehabilitation of criminal offenders. Chapter 364 does not apply to an applicant for a license or to a licensee where the underlying conduct on which the conviction is based would be grounds for denial, censure, suspension, or revocation of the license.

Subd. 11. Actions against lapsed license. If a license lapses, is surrendered, withdrawn, terminated, or otherwise becomes ineffective, the commissioner may institute a proceeding under this subdivision within two years after the license was last effective and enter a revocation or suspension order as of the last date on which the license was in effect, or impose a civil penalty as provided for in subdivision 6.

Subd. 12. Conditions of relicensure. A revocation of a license prohibits the licensee from making a new application for a license for at least two years from the effective date of the revocation. The commissioner may, as a condition of reapplication, require the applicant to obtain a bond or comply with additional reasonable conditions of licensure the commissioner considers necessary to protect the public.

History: 1987 c 336 s 2; 1989 c 330 s 2; 1990 c 415 s 1; 1991 c 306 s 1-6; 1992 c 564 art 1 s 2-8; 1993 c 145 s 1; 1993 c 204 s 3-7; 1993 c 361 s 3; 1994 c 385 s 3; 1996 c 384 s 1,2; 1996 c 439 art 1 s 4,5; art 2 s 1; 1997 c 7 art 2 s 7; 1999 c 137 s 1,2; 2000 c 483 s 1; 1Sp2001 c 9 art 16 s 1; 2002 c 379 art 1 s 113; 2004 c 285 art 4 s 1; 2004 c 290 s 20; 2009 c 37 art 2 s 5; 2010 c 384 s 2

CHAPTER 145C. HEALTH CARE DIRECTIVES

145C.02 Health care directive.

A principal with the capacity to do so may execute a health care directive. A health care directive may include one or more health care instructions to direct health care providers, others assisting with health care, family members, and a health care agent. A health care directive may include a health care power of attorney to appoint a health care agent to make health care decisions for the principal when the principal, in the judgment of the principal's attending physician, lacks decision-making capacity, unless otherwise specified in the health care directive.

History: 1993 c 312 s 3; 1998 c 399 s 12

145C.03 Requirements.
Subdivision 1. Legal sufficiency. To be legally sufficient in this state, a health care directive must:

(1) be in writing;
(2) be dated;
(3) state the principal's name;
(4) be executed by a principal with capacity to do so with the signature of the principal or with the signature of another person authorized by the principal to sign on behalf of the principal;
(5) contain verification of the principal's signature or the signature of the person authorized by the principal to sign on behalf of the principal, either by a notary public or by witnesses as provided under this chapter; and
(6) include a health care instruction, a health care power of attorney, or both.

***

Subd. 3. Individuals ineligible to act as witnesses or notary public. (a) A health care agent or alternate health care agent appointed in a health care power of attorney may not act as a witness or notary public for the execution of the health care directive that includes the health care power of attorney.

(b) At least one witness to the execution of the health care directive must not be a health care provider providing direct care to the principal or an employee of a health care provider providing direct care to the principal on the date of execution. A person notarizing a health care directive may be an employee of a health care provider providing direct care to the principal.

History: 1993 c 312 s 4; 1998 c 399 s 13

CHAPTER 325L. UNIFORM ELECTRONIC TRANSACTIONS ACT

***

325L.02 Definitions.
In this chapter:

***

(e) "Electronic" means relating to technology having electrical, digital, magnetic, wireless, optical, electromagnetic, or similar capabilities.

***

(g) "Electronic record" means a record created, generated, sent, communicated, received, or stored by electronic means.

(h) "Electronic signature" means an electronic sound, symbol, or process attached to or logically associated with a record and executed or adopted by a person with the intent to sign the record.

***

(n) "Security procedure" means a procedure employed for the purpose of verifying that an electronic signature, record, or performance is that of

a specific person or for detecting changes or errors in the information in an electronic record. The term includes a procedure that requires the use of algorithms or other codes, identifying words or numbers, encryption, or callback or other acknowledgment procedures.
***

History: 2000 c 371 s 2

325L.07 Legal Recognition of Electronic Records, Electronic Signatures, and Electronic Contracts.

(a) A record or signature may not be denied legal effect or enforceability solely because it is in electronic form.

(b) A contract may not be denied legal effect or enforceability solely because an electronic record was used in its formation.

(c) If a law requires a record to be in writing, an electronic record satisfies the law.

(d) If a law requires a signature, an electronic signature satisfies the law.

History: 2000 c 371 s 7

325L.09 Attribution and Effect of Electronic Record and Electronic Signature.

(a) An electronic record or electronic signature is attributable to a person if it was the act of the person. The act of the person may be shown in any manner, including a showing of the efficacy of any security procedure applied to determine the person to which the electronic record or electronic signature was attributable.

(b) The effect of an electronic record or electronic signature attributed to a person under paragraph (a) is determined from the context and surrounding circumstances at the time of its creation, execution, or adoption, including the parties' agreement, if any, and as otherwise provided by law.

History: 2000 c 371 s 9

325L.11 Notarization and Acknowledgment.

If a law requires a signature or record to be notarized, acknowledged, verified, or made under oath, the requirement is satisfied if the electronic signature of the person authorized to perform those acts, together with all other information required to be included by other applicable law, is attached to or logically associated with the signature or record.

History: 2000 c 371 s 11

CHAPTER 351. RESIGNATIONS, VACANCIES, REMOVALS

351.01 Resignations.

Subdivision 1. To whom made. Resignations shall be made in writing signed by the resigning officer:

(1) By incumbents of elective offices, to the officer authorized by law to fill a vacancy in such office by appointment, or to order a special election to fill the vacancy;

(2) By appointive officers, to the body, board, or officer appointing them, unless otherwise specially provided.

Subd. 2. When effective. Except as provided by subdivision 3 or other express provision of law or charter to the contrary, a resignation is effective when it is received by the officer, body, or board authorized to receive it.

Subd. 3. Contingent resignations prohibited; exception.(a) Except as provided in paragraph (b), no resignation may be made to take effect upon the occurrence of a future contingency. Statements explaining the reasons for a resignation must not be considered to be contingencies unless expressly stated as contingencies.

(b) A resignation may be made expressly to take effect at a stated future date. Unless it is withdrawn as provided under subdivision 4, a resignation is effective at 12:01 a.m. on the stated date.

Subd. 4. Withdrawal of resignation. A prospective resignation permitted by subdivision 3 may only be withdrawn by a written statement signed by the officer and submitted in the same manner as the resignation, and may only be withdrawn before it has been accepted by resolution of the body or board or before a written acceptance of the resignation by an officer authorized to receive it.

History: (6952) RL s 2666; 1987 c 200 s 2; 2004 c 293 art 2 s 44

CHAPTER 481. ATTORNEYS-AT-LAW

481.02 Unauthorized practice of law.

Subdivision 1. Prohibitions. It shall be unlawful for any person or association of persons, except members of the bar of Minnesota admitted and licensed to practice as attorneys at law, to appear as attorney or counselor at law in any action or proceeding in any court in this state to maintain, conduct, or defend the same, except personally as a party thereto in other than a representative capacity, or, by word, sign, letter, or advertisement, to hold out as competent or qualified to give legal advice or counsel, or to prepare legal documents, or as being engaged in advising or counseling in law or acting as attorney or counselor at law, or in furnishing to others the services of a lawyer or lawyers, or, for a fee or any consideration, to give legal advice or counsel, perform for or furnish to another legal services, or, for or without a fee or any consideration, to prepare, directly or through another, for another person, firm, or corporation, any will or testamentary disposition or instrument of trust serving purposes similar to those of a will, or, for a fee or any consideration, to prepare for another person, firm, or corporation, any other legal document, except as provided in subdivision 3.

***

Subd. 3. Permitted actions. The provisions of this section shall not prohibit:

(1) any person from drawing, without charge, any document to which the person, an employer of the person, a firm of which the person is a member, or a corporation whose officer or employee the person is, is a party, except another's will or testamentary disposition or instrument of trust serving purposes similar to those of a will;

(2) a person from drawing a will for another in an emergency if the imminence of death leaves insufficient time to have it drawn and its execution supervised by a licensed attorney-at-law;

***

(8) any person or corporation from drawing, for or without a fee, farm or house leases, notes, mortgages, chattel mortgages, bills of sale, deeds, assignments, satisfactions, or any other conveyances except testamentary dispositions and instruments of trust;

***

(14) the delivery of legal services by a specialized legal assistant in accordance with a specialty license issued by the Supreme Court before July 1, 1995;

Subd. 3a. Real estate closing services. Nothing in this section shall be construed to prevent a real estate broker, a real estate salesperson, or a real estate closing agent, as defined in section 82.17, from drawing or assisting in drawing papers incident to the sale, trade, lease, or loan of property, or from charging for drawing or assisting in drawing them, except as hereafter provided by the Supreme Court.

***

Subd. 8. Penalty; injunction. (a) Any person or corporation, or officer or employee thereof, violating any of the foregoing provisions shall be guilty of a misdemeanor; and, upon conviction thereof, shall be punished as by statute provided for the punishment of misdemeanors. It shall be the duty of the respective county attorneys in this state to prosecute violations of this section, and the district courts of this state shall have sole original jurisdiction of any such offense under this section.

(b) A county attorney or the attorney general may, in the name of the state of Minnesota, or in the name of the State Board of Law Examiners, proceed by injunction suit against any violator of any of the provisions above set forth to enjoin the doing of any act or acts violating any of said provisions.

(c) In addition to the penalties and remedies provided in paragraphs (a) and (b), the public and private penalties and remedies in section 8.31 apply to violations of this section.

History: (5687-1) 1931 c 114 s 1; 1959 c 476 s 1; 1969 c 9 s 87; 1974 c 406 s 49; 1981 c 168 s 1; 1983 c 247 s 173,174; 1986 c 444; 1987 c 377 s 6; 1988 c 695 s 3-5; 1991 c 299 s 1; 1992 c 376 art 1 s 1; 1992 c 497 s 1; 1992 c 591 s 1; 1993 c 321 s 1; 1994 c 502 s 1; 1994 c 568 s 2; 1997 c 174 art 12 s 70; 1999 c 86 art 1 s 74; 1999 c 199 art 2 s 19

CHAPTER 507. RECORDING AND FILING CONVEYANCES

507.093 Standards for Documents to be recorded or filed.

The following standards are imposed on documents to be recorded with the county recorder or the registrar of titles other than by electronic means as provided in section 507.24:

(1) The document shall consist of one or more individual sheets measuring no larger than 8.5 inches by 14 inches.

(2) The form of the document shall be printed, typewritten, or computer generated in black ink and the form of the document shall not be smaller than 8-point type.

(3) The document shall be on white paper of not less than 20-pound weight with no background color or images and, except for the first page, shall have a border of at least one-half inch on the top, bottom, and each side.

(4) The first page of the document shall contain a blank space at the top measuring three inches, as measured from the top of the page, and a border of one-half inch on each side and the bottom. The right half of the blank space shall be reserved for recording information and the left half shall be reserved for tax certification. Any person may attach an administrative page before the first page of the document to accommodate this standard. The administrative page may contain the document title, document date, and, if applicable, the grantor and grantee, and shall be deemed part of the document when recorded.

(5) The title of the document shall be prominently displayed at the top of the first page below the blank space referred to in clause (4), or on the administrative page.

(6) No additional sheet shall be attached or affixed to a page that covers up any information or printed part of the form.

(7) A document presented for recording must be sufficiently legible to reproduce a readable copy using the county recorder's or registrar of title's current method of reproduction.

History: 1996 c 338 art 3 s 1; 2000 c 275 s 2; 2002 c 365 s 1; 2005 c 156 art 2 s 40; 2006 c 222 s 1; 2008 c 238 art 3 s 11

***

507.0941 Definitions.

For purposes of sections 507.0941 to 507.0948:

(a) "Document" means information that is:

(1) inscribed on a tangible medium or that is stored in an electronic or other medium and is retrievable in perceivable form; and

(2) eligible to be recorded in the land records maintained by the recorder or registrar.

(b) "Electronic" means relating to technology having electrical, digital, magnetic, wireless, optical, electromagnetic, or similar capabilities.

(c) "Electronic document" means a document that is received by the recorder or registrar in an electronic form.

(d) "Electronic Real Estate Recording Commission" and "commission" mean the commission established by sections 507.0941 to 507.0948.

(e) "Electronic signature" means an electronic sound, symbol, or process attached to or logically associated with a document and executed or adopted by a person with the intent to sign the document.

(f) "Legislative Coordinating Commission" means the commission established by section 3.303.

(g) "Paper document" means a document that a recorder or registrar receives in a form that is not an electronic document.

(h) "Person" means an individual, corporation, business trust, estate, trust, partnership, limited liability company, association, joint venture, public corporation, government or governmental subdivision, agency, or instrumentality, or any other legal or commercial entity.

(i) "Recorder" means the county recorder for the county in which a document is received.

(j) "Registrar" means the registrar of titles for the county in which a document is received.

History: 2008 c 238 art 2 s 1

507.0943 Validity and time of recording of electronic documents.

(a) If a law requires, as a condition for recording, that a document be an original, on paper or another tangible medium, or in writing, the requirement is satisfied by an electronic document satisfying sections 507.0941 to 507.0948. If a law requires or refers to something related to tangible media including, without limitation, book, certificate, floor plan, page, volume, or words derived from them, the requirement or reference is satisfied by an electronic document satisfying sections 507.0941 to 507.0948.

(b) If a law requires, as a condition for recording, that a document be signed, the requirement is satisfied by an electronic signature.

(c) A requirement that a document or a signature associated with a document be attested, acknowledged, verified, witnessed, or made under oath is satisfied if the electronic signature of the person authorized to perform that act, and all other information required to be included, is attached to or logically associated with the document or signature. A physical or electronic image of a stamp, impression, or seal need not accompany an electronic signature.

***

507.24 Recordable, when.

Subdivision 1.General.

To entitle any conveyance, power of attorney, or other instrument affecting real estate to be recorded, it shall be legible and archivable, it shall be executed, acknowledged by the parties executing the same, and the acknowledgment certified, as required by law. All such instruments may be recorded in every county where any of the lands lie. If the conveyance, power of attorney, or other instrument affecting real estate is executed out of state, it shall be entitled to record if executed as above provided or according to the laws of the place of execution so as to be entitled to record in such place.

Subd. 2. Original signatures required.

(a) Unless otherwise provided by law, an instrument affecting real estate that is to be recorded as provided in this section or other applicable law must contain the original signatures of the parties who execute it and of the notary public or other officer taking an acknowledgment. However, a financing statement that is recorded as a filing pursuant to section 336.9-502(b) need not contain: (1) the signatures of the debtor or the secured party; or (2) an acknowledgment. An instrument acknowledged in a representative capacity as defined in section 358.41 on behalf of a corporation, partnership, limited liability company, or trust that is otherwise entitled to be recorded shall be recorded if the acknowledgment made in a representative capacity is substantially in the form prescribed in chapter 358, without further inquiry into the authority of the person making the acknowledgment.

(b) Any electronic instruments, including signatures and seals, affecting real estate may only be recorded in conformance with standards implemented by the Electronic Real Estate Recording Commission created under the Minnesota Real Property Electronic Recording Act, sections 507.0941 to 507.0948. The Electronic Real Estate Recording Commission created under the Minnesota Real Property Electronic Recording Act may adopt or amend standards set by the task force created in Laws 2000, chapter 391, and the Electronic Real Estate Recording Task Force created under section 507.094 and may set new or additional standards to the full extent permitted in section 507.0945. Documents recorded in conformity with the standards created as part of a pilot project for the electronic filing of real estate documents implemented by the task force created in Laws 2000, chapter 391, or by the Electronic Real Estate Recording Task Force created under section 507.094 are deemed to meet the requirements of this section.

(c) Notices filed pursuant to section 168A.141, subdivisions 1 and 3, need not contain an acknowledgment.

History: (8217) RL s 3348; 1947 c 566 s 2; 1973 c 9 s 3; 1998 c 262 s 7; 2001 c 195 art 1 s 20; 2002 c 365 s 2; 2003 c 90 s 2; 2005 c 4 s 120; 2005 c 156 art 2 s 42; 2007 c 148 art 2 s 70; 2008 c 238 art 3 s 12; 2008 c 341 art 3 s 1

CHAPTER 524. UNIFORM PROBATE CODE

524.2-502 Execution; witnessed wills.
Except as provided in sections 524.2-506 and 524.2-513, a will must be:
(1) in writing;
(2) signed by the testator or in the testator's name by some other individual in the testator's conscious presence and by the testator's direction or signed by the testator's conservator pursuant to a court order under section 524.5-411; and
(3) signed by at least two individuals, each of whom signed within a reasonable time after witnessing either the signing of the will as described in clause (2) or the testator's acknowledgment of that signature or acknowledgment of the will.

History: 1975 c 347 s 22; 1986 c 444; 1994 c 472 s 36; 2003 c 12 art 2 s 6

524.2-504 Self-proved will.
(a) A will may be contemporaneously executed, attested, and made self-proved, by acknowledgment thereof by the testator and affidavits of the witnesses, each made before an officer authorized to administer oaths

under the laws of the state in which execution occurs and evidenced by the officer's certificate, under official seal, in substantially the following form:

I, _____, the testator, sign my name to this instrument this ____ day of _____, and being first duly sworn, do hereby declare to the undersigned authority that I sign and execute this instrument as my will and that I sign it willingly (or willingly direct another to sign for me), that I execute it as my free and voluntary act for the purposes therein expressed, and that I am 18 years of age or older, of sound mind, and under no constraint or undue influence.

_____ Testator

We, _____, _____, the witnesses, sign our names to this instrument, being first duly sworn, and do hereby declare to the undersigned authority that the testator signs and executes this instrument as the testator's will and that the testator signs it willingly (or willingly directs another to sign for the testator), and that each of us, in the presence and hearing of the testator, hereby signs this will as witness to the testator's signing, and that to the best of our knowledge the testator is 18 years of age or older, of sound mind, and under no constraint or undue influence.

_____ Witness

_____ Witness

State of _____

County of _____

Subscribed, sworn to, and acknowledged before me by _____, the testator, and subscribed and sworn to before me by _____, and _____, witnesses, this ____ day of _____, _____.

(Signed) _____   (Stamp)

_____

(Official capacity of officer)

(b) An attested will may be made self-proved at any time after its execution by the acknowledgment thereof by the testator and the affidavits of the witnesses, each made before an officer authorized to administer oaths under the laws of the state in which the acknowledgment occurs and evidenced by the officer's certificate, under the official seal, attached or annexed to the will in substantially the following form:

MINNESOTA NOTARY LAW PRIMER

State of _____

County of _____

We, _____, _____, and _____, the testator and the witnesses, respectively, whose names are signed to the attached or foregoing instrument, being first duly sworn, do hereby declare to the undersigned authority that the testator signed and executed the instrument as the testator's will and that the testator had signed willingly (or willingly directed another to sign for the testator), and that the testator executed it as the testator's free and voluntary act for the purposes therein expressed, and each of the witnesses, in the presence and hearing of the testator, signed the will as witness and that to the best of the witness' knowledge the testator was at the time 18 years of age or older, of sound mind, and under no constraint or undue influence.

_____ Testator

_____ Witness

_____ Witness

Subscribed, sworn to, and acknowledged before me by _____, the testator, and subscribed and sworn to before me by _____, and _____, witnesses, this _____ day of _____, _____.

(Signed) _____   (Stamp)

_____

(Official capacity of officer)

(c) A signature affixed to a self-proving affidavit attached to a will is considered a signature affixed to the will, if necessary to prove the will's due execution.

History: 1975 c 347 s 22; 1979 c 240 s 1; 1986 c 444; 1994 c 472 s 37

CHAPTER 609. CRIMINAL CODE

609.65 False certification by notary public.

Whoever, when acting or purporting to act as a notary public or other public officer, certifies falsely that an instrument has been acknowledged or that any other act was performed by a party appearing before the actor or that as such notary public or other public officer the actor performed any other official act may be sentenced as follows:

(1) if the actor so certifies with intent to injure or defraud, to imprisonment for not more than three years or to payment of a fine of not more than $5,000, or both; or

(2) in any other case, to imprisonment for not more than 90 days or to payment of a fine of not more than $1,000, or both.

History: 1963 c 753 art 1 s 609.65; 1971 c 23 s 64; 1984 c 628 art 3 s 11; 1986 c 444; 2004 c 228 art 1 s 72 ■

About the NNA

Since 1957, the National Notary Association — a nonprofit educational organization — has served the nation's Notaries Public with a wide variety of instructional programs and services.

As the country's clearinghouse for information on Notary laws, customs and practices, the NNA® educates Notaries through publications, seminars, webinars, online training, annual conferences, its website and the NNA® Hotline that offers immediate answers to specific questions about notarization.

The Association is perhaps most widely known as the preeminent source of information for and about Notaries. NNA works include the following:

- *The National Notary*, a magazine for NNA members featuring how-to articles and practical tips on notarizing

- *Notary Bulletin*, an online newsletter that keeps NNA members and customers up to date on developments affecting Notaries, especially new state laws and regulations

- *Sorry, No Can Do!* series, four volumes that help Notaries explain to customers and bosses why some requests for notarizations are improper and cannot be accommodated

- *U.S. Notary Reference Manual*, an invaluable resource for any person relying upon the authenticity and correctness of legal documents

- *Notary Public Practices & Glossary*, a definitive reference book on notarial procedures and widely hailed as the Notary's bible

- State *Notary Law Primers*, short guidebooks that explain a state's Notary statutes in easy-to-understand language

- *The Notary Public Code of Professional Responsibility*, a comprehensive and detailed code of ethical and professional conduct for Notaries

- *The Model Notary Act*, prototype legislation conceived in 1973 and updated in 1984, 2002 and 2010 by an NNA-recruited panel of secretaries of state, legislators and attorneys, and regularly used by state legislatures in revising their Notary laws

- *Notary Signing Agent Training Course*, a manual covering every aspect of signing agent procedures that prepares candidates for the Notary Signing Agent Certification Examination developed by the NNA

- Public-service pamphlets informing the general public about the function of a Notary, including *What Is A Notary Public?* printed in English and Spanish

In addition, the NNA offers the highest quality professional supplies, including official seals and stamps, embossers, recordkeeping journals, jurat stamps, thumbprinting devices and Notary certificates.

Though dedicated primarily to educating and assisting Notaries, the NNA supports implementing effective Notary laws and informing the public about the Notary's vital role in modern society. ■

Index

A
Acknowledgment.... 8, **10–13**, 16, 38
Address change **6**
Advertising **44**, 55
Advice 10, **39**, 43–44, 55
Affidavit **15–19**, 38, 44
Affirmation 8–9, **14–22**, 25, 38–40
Apostille 48–50, *67*
Application, commission **2–7**, 54
Authentication 47–50
Authorized acts **8–9**
Awareness 22

B
Beneficial interest 25, **40–41**
Birth certificate 24
Blank certificate 35
Blank spaces 40, **45**
Bond **5**
Bureau of vital statistics 20

C
Certificate
   Authenticating **48–51**
   Commission 7
   Electronic 53–54
   Loose **34–35**
   Naturalization 45
Notary 9, 12–14, 17–19, 21,
   30–36, 54
Certified copy **19–21**, 30
Change of name or address **6–7**
Civil penalty or lawsuit 5, **56–57**
Commission certificate 7
Copy certification **19–21**
County court administrators'
   office 6, 48
Credible identifying witness .. 11, 16,
   23, **25–26**

D
Date
   Commission expiration . 36, 51, 53
   Document 28
   Notarization 31, 33, 53
Death certificate 20
Deposition 9, **18–19**
Disqualifying interest **40–41**

E
Electronic
   Notarization **50–54**
   Notary 54
   Record 20, 42, **51–54**
   Signature 31, 42, **51–52**
Employment, termination of ... 30, 38
Errors and omissions insurance 5

Page numbers listed in **bold** indicate where the most complete information on a subject can be found. *Italics* indicate pages where the statutes and state-published information pertaining to a subject are located.

93

MINNESOTA NOTARY LAW PRIMER

F
False certificate 54
Fees
    Application **4**, 7
    Authentication 48
    Notary **38–39**, 55
    Travel 39
Felony 54
Financial interest 25, **40–41**
Foreign language
    Advertising **44**, 55
    Documents 44–45
    Speakers 45

I
Identification 11, **22–27**, 43
Identification documents **23–24**
Immigration 45
Incomplete
    Certificate 35–36
    Document 45

J
Journal of notarial acts **26–30**
Jurat 8, 19, 32, 39
Jurisdiction **6**, 31, 33, 49

L
Laws, Notary 58–90
Liability 5, 57
Locus sigilli 32, **37**
Loose certificate **34–35**

M
Military-personnel Notaries 32,
                        46–47, 49, 53
Minnesota Statutes 58–90
Minors 43
Misconduct 2, 5, 35, **54–57**
Misdemeanor 35, 44, **54–56**

N
Name change **6–7**
National Notary Association ... **91–92**
Naturalization certificate 45
Nonresident 7
Notarial acts 8–22
Notary laws explained 2–55

Notary Public laws *58–90*

O
Oath 8–9, **14–22**, 25, 38–40
Oath of office 4

P
Penalties 39, 54–57
Personal appearance 13, 35
Personal knowledge of
    identity **23–24**
Photocopy 9, **19–21**, 46
Photograph 24–25
Practices and procedures 22–48
Prohibited acts .. 9, 39–41, 45, **54–55**
Proof of execution by subscribing
    witness 9
Protest 21–22
Public records 9, 20, 55

Q
Qualifications **2–3**

R
Reappointment 7
Reasonable care **57**
Recording commission **4**
Refusal of services **41**
Representative capacity **11–13**, 29
Residency requirement 2–3, 6
Resignation **7–8**
Revocation of commission 38,
                               55–57

S
Satisfactory evidence of identity ... 11,
                                 22–23
Scilicet 31
Services, Notary 38, 41–42
Signature 31–33, 33, 51
    Electronic **51–53**
    Mark, by 41–42
    Notary's 4, 9, 40, 55
    Proxy, by **42**
Signature witnessing 8, 11, **13–14**
Stamp 5–7, 31–32, **35–38**, 47,
                                   53, 56
Statement of particulars 32

INDEX

Statutes pertaining to
  notarization *58–90*
Subscribing witness 9

T

Term of office 6
Testimonium clause 32–33

U

Unauthorized acts **9**
Unauthorized practice of
  law **39–40**, 43–45, 55

V

Venue 19, **31**, 53
Verification upon oath or
  affirmation 8, **16–17**, 32, 38
Vital records 20

W

Willingness 22
Wills **43–44**
Witness 11, 16, **22–27**, 43–44
Witnessing a signature . 8, 11, **13–14**

Page numbers listed in **bold** indicate where the most complete information on a subject can be found. *Italics* indicate pages where the statutes and state-published information pertaining to a subject are located.

NOTES